W9-AYA-741

CAREER
STRATEGIES
for the
WORKING
WOMAN

ADELE SCHEELE, PH.D.

A FIRESIDE BOOK
Published by Simon & Schuster

New York   London   Toronto   Sydney   Tokyo   Singapore

FIRESIDE
Rockefeller Center
1230 Avenue of the Americas
New York, New York 10020

Copyright © 1994 by Adele Scheele

Designed by Richard Oriolo

Manufactured in the United States of America

ISBN: 0-671-88523-5

For my mother, Lillian Katz Marcus,
who works with dignity and discipline,
and loves and cares fiercely,
as life depends on it

CONTENTS

PART THREE
BUILDING RELATIONSHIPS WITH
CLIENTS AND COLLEAGUES

PART FOUR
TRIGGERING YOUR AMBITION

ACKNOWLEDGMENTS

The course of true change never runs smoothly. Since I began my column with *Working Woman* magazine in April 1990, the editors-in-chief I work with, and their larger visions, have changed. Kate White, the editor who revitalized the original *Working Woman*, invited me to become a regular columnist, and then left about a year later, taking her indelible magic to *McCalls*. *Newsweek*'s Lynn Povich, with her dedicated news orientation, was persuaded to replace her. The editors assigned to my column have also changed: Jani Scandori left New York to pursue a doctoral program in English at the University of Michigan; Pam Kruger, her colleague and friend, slid right over, juggling her own graduate courses and free-lance writing. *Working Woman*'s corporate events manager Margo Moore and corporate marketing director Barbara Cooper, together with the Fischer-Ross Speakers Group, have sent me out to hear and respond to readers at stimulating trade and business conferences. The *Working Woman* staff, under the able management of Rosemary Ellis, continues to produce a monthly miracle: a compelling, informative, and pioneering magazine about work.

My first book, *Skills for Success*, was published by William Morrow in hardcover, then by Ballantine in paperback in 1981— the dawning of an era of career how-to books. I found great encouragement from Ballantine's acquiring editor at that time, Marilyn Abraham, and wrote *Making College Pay Off* for her— with promises of delivering a third book. But she, too, moved upward and outward, and is now editor-in-chief of the Fireside and Touchstone imprints at Simon & Schuster. At her suggestion, along with votes of confidence from her senior editor Edward

Walters and his assistant Beverly Smith, I have collected over three years of my columns from *Working Woman* magazine. Together, *Working Woman* and the Fireside imprint have been an impressive combination for me. I am very grateful.

I am also indebted to my clients, the women and men who confide in me their career predicaments and ambitions. And, sometimes, I check my own advice against others' experience: Many thanks to my friends and colleagues—among them, Dr. Joye Weisel Barth, Cynthia Bernbach, Harriet Ehrlich, Claudia Gatlin, Valerie Geller, Phyllis and Marvin Levin, Sheena Paterson, Gail Rachlin, Mary Shourds, and Nancy Uridil.

A postscript is necessary. The long-accepted myth that men don't have career problems, and that only women's magazines need offer advice on resolving career dilemmas, has been exposed as fiction. The *Wall Street Journal*, for example, has inaugurated a "Managing Your Career" column that offers career advice. Finally, "careers" is now firmly established as a category—for both men and women—in magazines and newspapers, on bookstore shelves, and on television: NBC's *Weekend Today* has invited me to offer a career advice segment. But it's taken nearly twenty years to have the "how" of work so recognized and celebrated. It's surely welcome, for great work—how to do it, how to find it, and how to keep it—has been one of our best-kept secrets for far too long.

INTRODUCTION:
MAPPING INTENTIONS

How do we know whether we should re-enter, hang on, quit, transfer, move up, expand, or start anew at work? These are the real questions people ask me—whether in front of others in a conference hall or privately during a session, over the phone or face to face. We all crave finding the right work—work that we can succeed in and identify with.

Our search for work is something like our search for the perfect marriage, which old myths and fairy tales promised would end "happily ever after." Reality reveals marriage, like work, as the first step of a process that requires growth and change. We confront dilemmas at work that don't have easily charted solutions, just as we do during the course of a relationship. As in love, work relationships start out by engaging our interest, but making them last entails learning how to deal with disagreements, disappointment, and disasters.

Facing our inevitable career dilemmas evokes simultaneous feelings of despair and opportunity—the ever-present duality that accompanies change. To compound the problem, we're also wrestling with an unstable economy that has forced cutbacks, limitations, and structural reorganizations at the companies we work for. Even without the recession, our relationship to work would have changed. Our struggle to transform our careers, as well as the organizations we work for, is the result of a long-term structural change in the workplace that will continue well into the twenty-first century.

Evolution is never smooth or nice; it is nearly always experienced as chaos. Over the past three decades, we have witnessed the relentless growth of huge, hierarchical, greed-fed organizations that have expanded without reasonable limits. Today they are collapsing. The consequences of this collapse have been imposed on the millions of us who have lost our jobs; on those who have been caught up in the takeovers, mergers, and downsizings; on those who remain to clear up the debris and do the work of the missing legions.

And we still have to deal with our bosses, co-workers, clients, and suppliers, as well as our ever-changing, demanding families. The complexity of the workplace increases geometrically with the acceleration of the rate of change.

These changes are most noticeable in business; organizations are designed to respond to change. But, phoenix-like, a series of smaller, mobile, more flexible work units, both competitive and cooperative, are emerging. And we have to respond in kind, even when our natural instinct is to resist.

There have always been dilemmas in the workplace; today they come harder and faster. More than *problems* to be solved, *dilemmas* are complex issues that usually don't have neat resolutions. Unattended, they don't go away; they only get worse. Confronted head-on, they often bite back. Instead they call for reflection, exploration, and a strategic plan of attack.

Facing the unknown is the crux of change. Change causes pain. Change poses situations in which the next move, let alone the outcome, is not clear. Change forces options. Change inspires personal re-evaluations. And change fuels and manages hope.

We often don't know what to do, what to choose, what to ignore. We don't have established models for our new situations that tell us how to deal with these dilemmas. Without set formulas, we are forced into drawing new, sometimes tentative maps for unexpected and uncharted waters. We have to learn to steer ourselves. *Career Strategies for the Working Woman* is designed as a guide for the inevitable storms along the way.

I have been writing about work for more than twenty years, analyzing the meta-skills of life—the skills it takes to achieve goals as well as the skills it takes to solve dilemmas as they arise. For arise they surely will.

I know from my own experiences of coping with bad bosses, getting fired, leaving the known careers of teaching, counseling, and negotiating to forge a new career based only on my own developing interests and talents. While trying to find my own calling, I found that I could help others—not only find *their* own callings, but also negotiate the obstacles that appear on any career path.

What I learned and observed from others, plus the knowing that comes only from direct experience, the seat-of-my-own-pants process, has helped me to tap into the darkness and mystery of *dilemmas*, and illuminate the possibilities of coping, fighting back, and getting on with it.

The career strategies collected in this book come from me, not just as an objective observer, but as one who has continued to confront myself and my own career. And they come from the thousands of women and men whom I have had the privilege to counsel in corporations, professional associations, and universities, as well as in my private practice. And sometimes it's not so formal: I meet people who share their most profound dilemmas on planes, in theaters, in supermarket lines, and through the pages of *Working Woman* magazine. I listen and offer solutions that have been tried and have failed, that have been tried and have succeeded, or that are newly minted to meet the demands of the moment.

By sharing these stories, the true dilemmas and potentially rewarding strategies for resolution, I mean to provide a lore to guide us when we will inevitably confront a similar situation. But to reveal their identities—their names and organizations or industries—would backfire on those open enough to tell their stories, jeoporadizing their reputations, even their jobs. Their bosses, peers, and sometimes, their clients cannot tolerate either knowing that they felt hurt or angered or overlooked or that they took definite steps, manipulative ones, to reposition themselves.

Herein lies the double-edged sword of revealing career strategies: They need to be put into play or we lose our place, but they need to be invisible or we lose our respect. Therefore, I have protected people by changing or "fictionalizing" their names and businesses so that I can write freely about the need for recognizing how necessary career strategies are.

These strategies are based on survival skills, responses to situations that are never taught—not at home, nor in school, nor even, quite remarkably, on the job. Not knowing them takes its toll, not only in real terms such as career advancement, but also in more psychological and philosophical ones—in terms of defining oneself and making some sense of the world we live and work in. To find them, we have to follow the clues left by others who have figured out ways to meet their personal dilemmas, and to invent our own as we move courageously ahead.

All people who work need to work out their own career strategies, but women need to pay even more attention to the process than men. In facing our competition, finding favor from our bosses, firing up our ambition, we often find ourselves unprepared, tongue-tied, and self-doubting. As we are forced to come to terms with others, we find that first we have to come to terms with ourselves. Operating with less confidence than our male colleagues, we nonetheless have managed to place ourselves, more often than not, in the right place at the right time with both the experience and the connections to do the job. But to make our contributions count, to use our opportunities, to succeed over the long term, we need strategies that help us deal appropriately with our dilemmas.

Here's what it takes to transform yourself into the woman you want to be—and to claim the success you deserve.

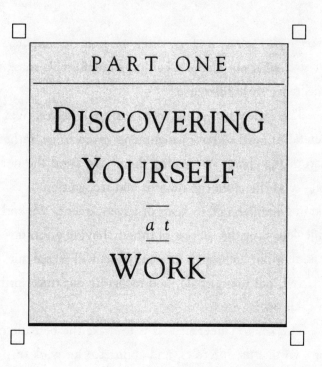

PART ONE

DISCOVERING YOURSELF

a t

WORK

We encode internal maps to our future. The power to start again, refire our desire, or rechart our plans lies within—if only we could read the tracings on those maps.

We hold the keys to managing the changes in our lives. The irony is that many of us are afraid to use the assets we have. We don't take ourselves seriously enough. We may complain about our lack of progress, but we hesitate to hold ourselves responsible. We fear achievement and success, we're afraid of claiming our place in the world, and too often we hide our talents, our strengths, our *life force* behind a comfortable mask of acceptance or indifference.

The reality is that we are cheating ourselves. We pretend to need to have assignments given to us, rather than taking charge of creating them. We avoid the hot seat—and therefore the rewards and recognition—feigning indifference to favor or advancement. We end up jealous over the success of others, having given up hope that our colleagues or supervisors will pierce our thin veil, our masquerade, and recognize our true worth on their own.

The key to career success is to make the best use of our own talents, interests, and abilities. Our work on ourselves begins with resolving the dilemmas that we may have inadvertently set up for ourselves. This part of the book focuses on what you can do to develop yourself into a more valuable, more productive, more successful person.

THE FLASH FACTOR: CAN YOU ELECTRIFY YOUR IMAGE?

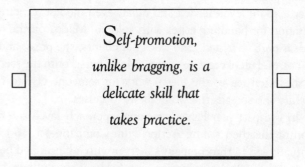

Self-promotion, unlike bragging, is a delicate skill that takes practice.

It's happened again: Diane Felder's colleague, Lisa Marks, has managed to steal the limelight. Felder and Marks are both account supervisors at a large West Coast public-relations firm. Marks oversees a paper-goods account, one of the firm's bread-and-butter clients—no showpiece in any sense. Felder's film and video client is more visible and potentially more profitable.

No matter. As Felder and Marks walk down the hallway with their boss, unit manager Jan Robertson, even Felder feels herself drawn in by Marks's enthusiasm about her progress on the paper-goods account and the national puzzle contest she has created. The truth is, Marks has done a good job. She's taken advantage of a boom market and has doubled what was a $500,000-a-year account. She's also managed to tout her own success in such a way that every senior manager recognizes it.

The hallway incident is just one more example of Mark's finesse: She recites her client's latest fan letter praising the agency for its work on the account. It doesn't sound like bragging coming from Marks—she drops remarks with such casual good humor—but she makes it clear whose work is responsible for the praise. Intimidated, Felder doesn't mention any of her own considerable accomplishments.

Felder and Marks have similar PR expertise and backgrounds, although Felder, with a master's degree, has the educational advantage. The real difference between the two, however, is style. Felder is more level-headed and quiet, even modest, despite her reputation for handling crises with aplomb. Marks, on the other hand, is pure charisma. She woos her clients, the press, and her own bosses. Full of creative energy, Marks bursts onto the scene—but she often leaves the messy work for someone else to clean up while she spreads the word about successes.

In the past year Felder's rational approach saved the reputation of the then failing Action Film Company—a move that eventually led to the company's merger with a bigger and better-financed Australian corporation. But Felder is tired of being seen simply as a dependable worker and great troubleshooter. Now the film company, with a beefed-up budget and a new video division that's expected to bring in hefty bonuses from licensed merchandise, has become one of the firm's plum accounts. Felder has big plans and knows that pulling them off will be the stepping-stone for more power and prestige at the firm. She'll have an opportunity to prove herself as a creative thinker—one of the most valued roles in her office.

□   # THE SUBTLE ART OF   □
SELF-PROMOTION

Felder has to persuade Robertson not to switch accounts on her—and to start seeing her in a different light. To do this, she must treat herself as her own best client. Her first move:

walking into Robertson's office first thing Monday morning, a time when she's found her boss to be most receptive.

FELDER: Hi. How was your weekend?

ROBERTSON: Busy. My in-laws dropped by and I had a rush on the new dog-food account.

FELDER: Sounds like just what you needed! *(Pauses.)* Oh, by the way, I had dinner with Bill Stone from Action Film on Friday. He's great. You know, I think this video campaign is going to be more profitable than the movie contract was. We agreed on the new campaign in about ten minutes.

ROBERTSON: Great. I want the account to bring in more film business.

FELDER: I have a million ideas for the project. I think going after merchandise will bring in a fortune for them. Stone gobbled up the idea, especially when I told him that Joyful Toys was biting.

ROBERTSON: Well, that's nice to hear . . .

FELDER: Jan, I've thought about your suggestion that I switch accounts with Lisa. But I'd really like to keep Action Film. We have a good thing going. Stone trusts me and loves the campaign I've proposed. And I think I've figured out a way to use the account to stir up more film work. Here's a memo I drafted over the weekend about my idea.

ROBERTSON: Fantastic. *(Takes memo.)* But look, I didn't suggest the switch as a demotion. I just thought you'd be more in sync with Ready Paper.

FELDER: You know I think the world of Lisa, and I'm always available to brainstorm with her, if she wants my input. I just feel my talents would be better utilized with Action Film. I want this chance to show you that I can make a hot account even hotter.

Felder has stated her case without attacking Robertson or Marks. She's presented herself as a team player who's creative and simpatico with her client. And she's been careful to tout her command of the secondary markets and to show she can plan for future business. By telling Robertson about her success and ambition, she has created a different aura about herself, one that's professional, competent, *and* magnetic—just what Robertson will reward.

□   □

But now Felder may not get the chance. As they turn the corner, Robertson says, "What would you two think of swapping accounts? Lisa, your energy might help us pull in more film business. And Diane, I think you'll be able to give Ready Paper a nice, steady hand." Marks is flattered by her boss's confidence in her ability to garner future film business. But Felder is outraged and feels she is being subtly pushed off the promotion track. She plays for a little more time by saying, "Let me think about it and get back to you."

STRATEGY

FELDER'S boss is smart enough to know that while hard, competent work is important, what's done is not so important as how the client *feels* about what's done. Robertson sees Marks's ability to magnify the results of an account, which in turn attracts new business. Although she values Felder's work, she doesn't hear her ambition or see her flair and assumes it is less than Marks's. Asking Marks and Felder to swap accounts is not an unjustified management decision, based on the facts as she sees them. It's up to Felder to change Robertson's perception of those facts.

Felder stands to lose her account and, possibly, a chance for a promotion. Understandably she feels both envy and contempt for Marks. But rather than despair, Felder has to transform herself into a more powerful and competitive professional and develop her self-presentation skills. If she doesn't, she risks falling into what I call the *Sustainer's Trap:* doing her job perfectly and expecting others to applaud her worthiness. That's a big mistake.

Where did Felder get that expectation? Where all of us do—at school, where the right answers are rewarded with the best grades. At work the rules are different; they are more experimental, less predictable, and far more interesting.

Remember the philosopher's dilemma: "If a tree falls in a forest but no one is there to hear it, does it make a sound?" Felder may do a great job, but if her boss, her boss's boss, and her clients don't hear about it, she hasn't made a sound. What we perceive becomes our notion of reality, whether or not it's based on fact. Felder is in an industry where charisma counts. And she works for a boss who values it. So it's time for her to lift the veil of modesty and start promoting herself.

Unlike bragging, which is easy as well as annoying, self-promotion is a subtle skill. And like any skill, it requires a good deal of practice—trial and error—to learn how to make a strong point without coming on *too* strong. Marks obviously has got the technique down, so rather than resent her, Felder should make an effort to learn from her. Take that fateful hallway talk: Felder could have let Marks finish her story, complimented her on her success, then shared her own. But instead of actively participating, Felder saw Marks as a sort of teacher's pet and withdrew.

What can Felder do now? She can rehearse her plans for success and relay them casually—but enthusiastically—to Robertson when she drops by her office. She should keep her boss abreast of even minor successes. Send memos? Of course—to Robertson, and, if appropriate in the corporate culture, she should pass on copies to Robertson's superiors. If Felder has gone beyond the call of duty, she should send her boss a quick "Just to keep you up to date" or "Thought you'd like to know" note, or drop in and tell her.

Felder should also casually mention her achievements to friends in the industry and try to get the get the good news picked up in trade journals, thereby making herself more visible to senior management. And she should do favors for others when possible; they're usually returned.

The key is to use humor, optimism, and enthusiasm—and to be generous to those who have helped you. Of course, once Felder gets people to think of her as an achiever, her image will be a lot easier to keep intact. After all, success does breed success.

YOU'RE JEALOUS:
WHAT CAREER ENVY
REALLY MEANS

No one wants to admit to
envying a colleague, but those
who do can discover the truth about
their own ambitions.

Laurie MacIntosh picked up the memo just as it was tossed into her box. It was from the chief administrator of the hospital. "I am pleased to report that Marianne Miller has been promoted to director of training, effective September 15," the memo began. "As you all know, Marianne has been doing a superb job . . ." MacIntosh's hands were shaking; she felt numb.

MacIntosh and Miller started out together fifteen years ago as RNs-in-training. They were friends and equals until about three years ago, when Miller abandoned nursing and asked for a transfer into the education department as a training assistant. At the time, Miller said she was tried of nursing, particularly of fighting the constant losing battles with doctors, and she wanted to move into a field where she would command more repect and greater pay. MacIntosh never suspected what would follow.

The two stopped talking soon after Miller was transferred. She had turned into a master politicker, volunteering to be the hospital's representative at the chamber of commerce and helping organize the hospital's annual conference on medical ethics. While MacIntosh worked ungodly hours—sometimes putting in seventy-hour weeks—catering to demanding patients and insensitive doctors, Miller was serving on committees and networking with the administrators. It worked. Now Miller would probably be making three times what MacIntosh was earning as a nurse, and she'd have the authority to make important changes rather than having to submit to doctor's whims.

It was so unfair. Miller wasn't any smarter than MacIntosh, just more ruthless, perhaps. MacIntosh fantasized about leaving nursing, but at her age, thirty-two, she was too old to start in an entry-level position, and anyway, what department would take her? Besides, she told herself, nursing was a noble profession, not to be abandoned for selfish reasons.

☐ # THE SIGNS OF ENVY ☐

It is hard to recognize your own jealousy, particularly when it involves a work associate. People often rationalize or deny their envious feelings in order to avoid the unpleasant experience of examining their emotions. Here are some questions to help you figure out your underlying motivation.

- Do you constantly compare yourself with others?
- Have you ever belittled their accomplishments or talents?
- Do you feel upset when they are promoted or take up new challenges?
- Have you ever been tempted to badmouth or sabotage someone?

If you answered "yes" to at least two of these questions, you are hiding from something, and it is probably envy. People who feel professional envy are usually dissatisfied with their own lot because they have not realized their ambitions. As a result they are plagued by feelings of failure. What you need to do is face your unfulfilled dreams. Once you have done so you will have freed yourself to act on them and to propel yourself forward. Here are some questions that will help you start that process of self-exploration.

- Who did I wish I could be when I was young?
- Should I act on it?
- Whom do I wish I were more like now?
- How can I achieve that?
- What attributes does my subject of envy have that I want for myself?
- What steps can I take to develop these qualities?
- Can I achieve something similar for myself during this coming year?
- If so, what actions do I need to take this month?
- To whom can I turn for support?

☐   ☐

STRATEGY

MACINTOSH can castigate Miller for "selfishness" and justify her own inability to take risks as being principled, but the truth is, she is envious. Labeling Miller a "hustler" is a lot easier than facing her own jealousy.

Envy is an emotion we all do our best to deny. One of the seven deadly sins, which in Christian doctrine lead to spiritual death, envy seems shameful. Yet those who dare to recognize it in themselves can be freed from it and act on it. Instead of hiding from their feelings, these people can use envy as a motivational whip—not to flog themselves but to spur themselves on to make the changes they desperately want to make.

But how do you learn to see through your rationalizations

and recognize that you are jealous? If you are following your dream, then you should, for the most part, be happy when a colleague or friend succeeds. You should feel it is a confirmation that life is fair when others' good works are rewarded.

If you feel they don't deserve their good fortune, you may, perhaps, look on with disappointment, but you won't attribute their success to their "good luck" and curse your lack of it. And you certainly won't feel the kind of anger MacIntosh is experiencing. When these kinds of harsh feelings arise, it is a surefire sign that you consider yourself a failure but haven't admitted how or why. It is critical that you confront your feelings of failure. Only when you acknowledge them will you be able to discover the answers that will help build success.

MacIntosh is clearly angered by Miller's rapid rise in salary and authority because she herself feels stagnant and frustrated in her job. They both started out in the same place, though MacIntosh got stuck and Miller didn't. Miller took risks and eventually got herself into a more satisfying position. Out of her fear of losing a secure but unsatisfying job, MacIntosh took refuge in self-righteousness and tried to convince herself that Miller's corporate savvy was unethical. Had MacIntosh been brave enough to read her own feelings, she might have interpreted them for what they were—a sign of her dependency and fear—and might have been moved to take action.

Whom you envy and what you envy will tell you a great deal about your secret ambitions. For example, suppose you are a private investment adviser and envy the CPA who works at an accounting firm. You need to ask yourself what you envy. Is it her salary? Her power? The answers to these questions will go a long way to pinpointing your dissatisfaction and helping you figure out what it is you want.

Career envy poses particularly difficult problems for women. Too often bright, talented, and ambitious women have accepted the old societal myth that women are intellectually inferior. So if asked what they want, they will say they don't know. They do know, of course, but they have repressed their desires. Unconsciously they feel they don't deserve success because they don't feel smart enough, capable enough, or experienced enough. Secretly they are waiting for an authority figure—a boss or a mentor—to give them permission to claim their lives and validate their success. But even when they do get a promotion or a pat on the back, they can doubt the worthiness of their achievements and try to build themselves up by denigrating someone else's accomplishments. In doing so, they shirk their responsibility to themselves.

MacIntosh wants to leave nursing but hasn't figured out where to transfer her energies. I don't know what her next step is either. She will need time to discover her untapped interests and talents. That will mean soul searching—closely examining the reasons for her envy and recalling old, suppressed dreams. While she is working on that, she can also use her time to develop her skills and boost her confidence so she is ready for the next step in her career. For example, she might join and lead a nurses' association or get involved in a community group. She could pursue an advanced degree. She should also congratulate Miller and use her friend's success to inspire herself.

Envy hurts because we see our missed opportunities reflected in someone else's face. If we refuse to recognize our reflection, and deny that it is our own, we lose ourselves. But if we recognize it, we can begin to find out who we are, and who we really want to be.

PIGEONHOLED:
HOW TO BREAK OUT

□ *If you don't like how you are perceived, you've got to change your image. It's easier than you think.* □

Carol Ott, vice president of financial affairs at a consumer-goods company, watched in pain as Janet Goodman, a vice president of strategic planning, gave a dazzling performance at a staff meeting. Once again, with seemingly no effort or preparation, Goodman delivered sharp, off-the-cuff insights and ideas. Everyone was impressed and seemed to get a charge from her creative energy. Except Ott. She spent the meeting wishing she could be more like Goodman.

Ott is seen as a numbers cruncher: smart, conscientious, and reliable, but not the one to inspire a staff with her foresight and imagination. Until this meeting, Ott has told herself that she doesn't care that she isn't perceived as "creative." She doesn't mind that she isn't one of the people chosen for the glamorous projects. After all, she has a relatively senior position in the company, she is respected by her peers, and the work she does is considered by all to be important.

But during the meeting Ott had one of those life-altering realizations. She isn't merely low-profile—she is a drudge. While Goodman performs in Technicolor, Ott is in black and white. It is not a pleasant picture, yet Ott wonders whether she can change it. She has ideas, but she is shy. She feels ill at ease speaking up in meetings. She is most comfortable in groups, listening and observing.

A friend of Ott's had once gone to an image consultant and found that it helped her enormously. She suggested that Ott do the same. "You'll feel like a new person!" she said. Ott wants to change her image, but is that possible? And is it even really necessary? After all, perhaps her colleagues don't judge her as critically as she judges herself. And even if they do, maybe there isn't anything wrong with being perceived as a numbers cruncher.

☐ A MANAGERIAL MAKEOVER ☐

You've been pegged, and the image they have of you is holding you back. Can you change their picture of you? Absolutely. But it will take hard work.

Step 1. Examine the various criticisms of you. In your performance reviews, consider the areas that have been listed as those in which you need to improve. What subtle messages have people sent you about how they view you? If everyone's vision of you is the same, the problem is probably with you, not with them.

Step 2. The most common labels with which people are pegged are "too detail-oriented," "too technical," "numbers cruncher," "too junior," and "not a leader." Underlying these criticisms is the sense that you are not fulfilling your managerial role in the company.

You may feel, as many women unconsciously do, that you somehow do not deserve the position. Your lack of confidence may relate to some past trauma, perhaps when you tried to seize the initiative but didn't succeed. Recognize what you fear, and take small steps to overcome it.

Step 3. Keep an hourly log for a week. Write down the activities you engage in, the orders you delegate, and how you check up on their follow-through. Take a management course and read a few management books for inspiring ideas to try. Rate your success to see which ideas help you move into the role of manager and which keep you stuck in the role of employee.

Step 4. Find another executive with a managerial style you admire and ask how he or she learned to manage so effectively. You might also try to use this person as a mentor, or search out someone else for that role. (You may even want to hire a career or management consultant to coach you.) Show your mentor your log and ask for input. What other ideas does he or she think you should try? Once you begin experimenting and taking risks, you will find yourself assuming the role that you always desired—and deserved.

☐   ☐

STRATEGY

REALITY *versus* perception. Ott is struggling with a basic philosophical dilemma—who am I, and who do I want to be? But in this case, studying philosophy won't help.

In the workplace, reality is simple—it is our shared perceptions. We are what people around us think we are. Some people, like Ott, may argue that they have been unfairly pegged. They've been classified as followers when they can lead; detail-oriented rather than visionary; or, as in Ott's case, number crunchers instead of creative thinkers. It is true—people do have a tendency to pigeonhole one another. No malice is involved; we do it simply because it is so easy to do. And while first impressions often can be off the mark, they tend to be corrected in the long run as people see your behavior on a day-to-day basis.

But what do you do if your image of how you want to be is at odds with what those around you see? You change, particularly if you feel the image is holding back your career, as it is in Ott's case. It's not so impossible as it sounds. In fact, people do it all the time.

The classic instance of image changing involves one who starts as an entry-level employee and works her way up to a senior position. Often co-workers persist in seeing the person as a junior employee. But from what I've observed, the fault lies with the person in most cases. She hasn't changed her behavior to suit her new position. She is still hesitant, tentative, and eager for approval when she should be decisive and authoritative. As a result, her colleagues continue to see her—and treat her—as a subordinate.

There is no such thing as a fixed, "true" self. We all behave differently in different situations. If you view yourself as a collection of selves, change will be possible.

Some of you will no doubt protest: Can you really change your personality? Isn't it something you are born with? Goodman's pleasure lies in generating new ideas and brainstorming with others. Ott's has been derived from implementing others' creative ideas. But that is only one aspect of their respective selves.

Different situations demand different responses. We are constantly adjusting our behavior and ourselves to fit the situation. Think about it: We speak to our parents differently than we do to our children, or our staff, or our bosses. We might bravely intervene in public to prevent a social disaster but be gripped with anxiety over the need to confront a colleague. Similarly, we might have no problem making smooth business presentations but feel overwhelmed at the prospect of throwing a dinner party for our boss. Who we are is a collection of selves—some more experienced and polished then others. If we view ourselves this way, there is more promise of change than if we cling to some absolute "self" as if it were a Procrustean mold that we must torture ourselves to fit.

But Ott is right to be skeptical. Change does not come easily or without extraordinary effort. It isn't as simple as dressing up or learning a few management tricks. What is required is facing your fears so you can change your behavior. In her own case, Ott isn't afraid of using her intellect so much as assuming her place among her peers. For some reason—it may be related to a childhood trauma or having once failed in a social engagement—Ott shrinks from the spotlight. She blames it on a personality characteristic, shyness, to cover up her fear of coming out of her shell. How can I tell? She would not feel so aggrieved and be so conflicted if she wasn't holding herself back from something she yearns for. Ott is caught in a bad habit, hoping to fit in by fading out; she won't take the risk of being the center of attention. Stuck in the dark, that limited role she calls home, Ott comforts herself by claiming it is her true, immutable self. But she is all wrong.

She can have a brighter, more creative, and fulfilling career. She has already taken the first step—acknowledging what she wants to be. Now she needs to take the steps to become that person. This means daring to suggest an idea at a meeting or offering her thoughts about others' ideas. She might also consider going to a career or management consultant to learn how to open a meeting, make a presentation, and manage feedback. The consultant would help her rehearse so that she will appear more confident, and eventually become so.

Facing her weaknesses and fears will be a difficult process. Unfortunately, changing an image isn't so easy as buying a new wardrobe or getting a new haircut. There aren't any shortcuts or easy cures. But the payoff is a career that will satisfy for a lifetime.

FEELING INVISIBLE? HERE'S HOW TO GET CLOUT

> Cultivating influence
> is one of the most difficult
> skills to master. It's also one
> of the most essential.

"Hey, Moorfield, make something *happen*. Stop neatening your lists!" Greg Hull, a colleague in the university development office, was teasing Cheryl Moorfield. She laughed, but the joke stung. She realized that her performance wasn't stellar, not because she was doing anything poorly, but because she just wasn't "making things happen." Like Hull does.

His remarks jolted Moorfield into a reassessment of her performance. How did Hull manage to get his fund-raising plans off the ground, winning the approval of the university president and wealthy alumni? Hers puttered along, sitting on someone's desk for weeks, sometimes months, only to be rejected.

Hull and Moorfield started out as equals: Both got fine undergraduate and graduate educations, first jobs at small liberal-arts colleges, then fund-raising posts at major universities. They were hired at the same level—assistant director of development—but sometime during the least two years, Hull pulled ahead.

Hull, who had maneuvered his way into the social world of the university's most important donors, had persuaded a few wealthy alumni to establish special departmental scholarships and to subsidize the salaries of some star scholars the university was afraid of losing. His work has begun to gain notice—and acclaim—from the heavy hitters, too. Just last week the local newspaper ran a glowing, full-page article about him, calling him one of the university's "best assets."

It isn't fair. Hull isn't more talented or smarter than Moorfield, just better at playing the game. He's a politicker who became successful by kowtowing to key alumni and the school's head honchos and showering them with compliments. "Great suit!" he'll say. "Is that a Chanel?"

What's worse, it works.

Moorfield cannot bring herself to behave that way. She is serious about her work and has serious ideas, ideas that would not only raise money but might even enhance the university's reputation and transform the way it does business. Specifically, she wants to expand on the Great Books concept and offer top executives special seminars on literature and philosophy, taught by the university's leading academics. Moorfield's research has revealed that executives in their forties and fifties would welcome an opportunity to study. Once they began, she reasons, their appreciation of the university would grow, and so would their contributions; they might even be inclined to enter into joint research projects with the school.

The idea exhilarates Moorfield, but she can't figure out how to propose it successfully. Her word carries little weight with her superiors. Is there any way to change that?

MAKING THEM LISTEN: SIX WAYS

Are your memos gathering dust in someone's in-basket? Is your advice being ignored? Can't get your projects approved? You need influence. Here are six ways to get it.

1. *Develop your talents and turn yourself into an expert.* Are you great at digging out facts? Or do you have a natural gift for socializing? Build on your strengths and people will begin to turn to you.

2. *Study the people upon whom the leaders in your company rely.* You can learn from them. What do they provide, and can you offer the same skills and knowledge? Could these people help you as advisers or mentors?

3. *Provide your bosses with what they need to thrive.* Is it marketing information, strategic planning, or numbers crunching? Find out what your supervisors need to be successful and give them what you can. They'll be grateful and will lean on you in the future if you help them.

4. *Read profiles and biographies of achievers.* Pay close attention to the opportunities they seized and the people who helped them. Then apply that knowledge to your own life. Are there opportunities in your office that you should be acting on? Is there any way in which you can assist an achiever in your own company?

5. *Make yourself visible.* Network, build relationships with high-ranking people in your company, speak up at meetings, and volunteer to serve on interoffice task forces. Write memos that show off your knowledge. The more

people who are aware of you and your good work, the better your chances that they will rely on you.

6. *Practice in a safe environment.* Join professional and civic organizations and test these techniques to see which work best for you.

☐   ☐

Like most of us, Moorfield yearns to make significant contributions and to be recognized for them. But she fails to comprehend what she needs to make things happen: a superior who values her know-how and will provide her with opportunities to use it. In short, she needs influence.

Some people are lucky enough to have high-ranking jobs, such as president, that automatically confer influence. Sheer wealth, of course, acts as a magnet, as does a naturally charismatic personality. But most people have to work hard to gain whatever influence they have. And how do they do that? They make sure their bosses know precisely how valuable they are. They provide them with key information, effective strategies, and whatever else the higher-ups might need to succeed.

To rise in an organization, you also must rise in the estimation of the top brass. A simple fact. But I have seen many people bypassed or fired because they failed to recognize that they need to do *more* than their jobs. They need to make themselves— and their good work—known.

For women, seeking influence can be a psychologically difficult task. Many, like Moorfield, try to win approval by playing it safe. Historically women have had to prove themselves over and over again simply to be taken seriously by their employers. Men, on the other hand, are automatically deemed competent and have to prove themselves losers or thieves before they are dismissed. Unfair, but true. A dilemma then builds: How can women prove themselves capable of belonging when their bosses instinctively—and usually unconsciously—doubt them? Grateful to be included in the game, many try not to call attention to themselves. They don't dare propose a plan that might fail. But if they don't take that chance, they will go nowhere.

Instead of denigrating Hull, Moorfield needs to study and learn from him. He understands one of the critical ways people gain influence—through forging alliances with those at the top. He has made himself visible, and so should Moorfield. If she doesn't like Hull's approach to building relationships—sycophancy—then she needs to adopt an approach she feels more comfortable with. Many people have increased their influence by taking on the projects that nobody else, including their bosses, wanted. While these tasks can involve extra work that is often quite tedious, the willingness to help usually pays off.

If that doesn't appeal to Moorfield, she can volunteer to serve on interdepartmental task forces that deal with the issues in which she is most interested. She also could speak out in staff meetings, but only when she has something to say and is certain her ideas will make a valuable contribution. Every project she undertakes should be approached seriously, as if she were presenting it directly to the president.

The Great Books idea sounds intriguing, but to overcome her fear of risk and her superiors' resistance to her ideas, she needs to prepare, even overprepare. The fact that her idea has never been tried before (at least, not at her university) requires that she be especially persuasive. Some of the most successful women I know are obsessive planners; they make sure they have worked out every possible hitch before they publicly propose anything. As a result, they are seen as reliable, conscientious, and capable.

To avoid disasters, Moorfield should speak to conference planners and other people who have organized weekend events at universities for high-level corporate executives. She should invite their advice, as well as that of her superiors. When she finally presents her plan, it must be fully developed, and she must make a great sales pitch, giving the projected outcome first. Since

Moorfield's plan requires a harmonious relationship between the university and the business community, she might consider lobbying for permission to establish a committee of business and university leaders so they can develop the idea together.

Moorfield may not succeed at this secret dream of hers. Developing influence requires practice, and she'll probably hit a few wrong notes. But she needs to keep trying—harder, better, and sometimes even differently. It's time for Moorfield and women like her to stop just doing their jobs. They need to dance to the organizational anthem. Once they learn the rhythm, they will be able to create the special role they want.

You've Failed:
Can You Bounce Back?

> The key isn't to
> avoid setbacks but to
> make them work
> for you.

Deborah Davis's boss broke the news simply enough. In a meeting of ad-sales managers at the newspaper chain, the boss, Ann Geiger, casually mentioned that Davis's top client was being assigned to another salesperson because the account needs some "new blood." And that was that. No more discussion. Davis was out of the picture.

Dumbstruck, Davis managed to stumble through the rest of the day, tidying up her desk and writing "to do" lists. The next day she called in sick and tried to piece together what had happened. Looking back, she realized that she and Geiger hadn't had an in-depth conversation in months. She had interpreted Geiger's coolness as nothing worse than distraction; now she recognized that Geiger had been sending her a message. But why would Geiger be dissatisfied with her work?

In the three years that Davis had managed the account, the client had never once cut back on its ad pages, despite the fact that it was suffering from the worst recession to hit the industry in years. Of course, the company had *threatened* to pull ads twice in the past year, but Davis had convinced them to hang on.

Priding herself on being direct and open in her dealings with others, Davis had relayed these threats and confessed her doubts to Geiger. Could that very forthrightness have been her mistake? Allan Singer, the colleague now assigned to the account, talked himself up so much that he made even his most unsuccessful sales calls sound like feats of great genius. Davis had always had contempt for people like that, but now she wondered whether her candor hadn't worked against her. What should she do? Never having experienced such a big failure before, she was embarrassed and just wanted to hide.

☐   # GETTING BACK ON TRACK: ☐
A QUIZ

Sometimes you must learn the hard way what went wrong. Take this quiz to test your ability to make things right again.

1. *You are dressed down by your boss in private. You:*
   A. Blow off steam by telling co-workers.
   B. Forget what happened—you know you're good at what you do.
   C. Analyze your boss's criticism and vow to follow her suggestions.
   ANSWER: C. While listening to your boss's negative comments will be painful, it's your best chance to learn from your mistake, and ultimately it will help improve your relations. Choice A is a common but childish response and the least productive of the three. As for B, denial can be an effective coping mechanism in the short run, but eventually it will lock you into the losing position of adversary to your supervisor.

2. *You call your most important client by the wrong name.*
   After apologizing, you:
   A. Feel so terrible that you go to your boss and promise that you'll never do it again.
   B. Put the incident out of your mind—everyone makes mistakes.
   C. Go to your colleagues for comfort.

ANSWER: B. If you've never had this problem before, forgive yourself for this one gaffe. As for A and C, it is not wise to tell people about every slip you make; it will only serve to damage your image. (*One caveat:* Tell your boss if you are fairly certain that someone else will otherwise.)

3. *You know you cannot bounce back when:*
   A. Nothing you do pleases your boss.
   B. Your best account has just been taken away from you.
   C. You feel you aren't able to perform up to your own standards.

ANSWER: A. If your boss consistently maligns your work, you have to move on to maintain your reputation— and your self-esteem. No matter how talented you are, you need confirmation and support from your boss in order to thrive. If you chose B, you are taking one setback too much to heart; everyone fails once in a while. And C indicates that you may be your own worst critic; if so, work on improving your self-image.

☐   ☐

STRATEGY

THERE are two basic kinds of failure. There are the private ones—your boss reprimands you in her office or you repeatedly call an important client by the wrong name—which only a select few know about. And then there are the public disasters, such as a demotion or a firing, which cannot be kept secret from your colleagues no matter how hard you try.

In both cases, it's natural to feel humiliated, but when everyone knows about your setback, it can seem like your entire office becomes a Greek chorus, chanting over and over in your ear, "You've failed!" Your initial response may be to slide into a maelstrom of shame and depression. Then you may have an impulse to hide at home, like Davis, or to redouble your efforts to prove the others wrong. While these reactions are to be expected, giving in to them would be destructive.

Instead, you need to figure out what went wrong and what you might have done, and can still do, to remedy the situation. In so doing, you will be better equipped for your next disappointment, for there will inevitably be another. Failing is a part of being a professional—only those who don't take risks escape it, and as a result, they never truly succeed. The question, then, is not how to avoid failure but how to learn from it so you don't make the same mistake twice.

Davis has taken the right approach so far. She is expressing her dismay privately and attempting to analyze what she did that might have led to her losing the account, and why she didn't see the signs. Demotions do not occur without many hints beforehand. Geiger, for instance, had been avoiding Davis for months. If Davis had recognized that message and approached her boss, she may well have been able to allay Geiger's concerns—or at least identify them.

Davis still can, and should, do that. As soon as she feels she can handle it emotionally, she should schedule a meeting with Geiger to find out the areas in which she needs to improve and which projects she should take on to gain these skills. She may be surprised at what she learns. She might discover, for example, that she lost the account because a new department head requested the change, perhaps for a reason unrelated to her performance.

In any event, Davis has to give up her naive eagerness to confess her flaws and misgivings. I've noticed in my practice that many women feel a similar obligation to be "candid." Having internalized stereotypes of female inferiority, we are quick to accept culpability. Men find it easier to deny personal or emotional responsibility and to project blame onto others. When men's projects flop, they are more likely to see it as a result of economic factors, an overly critical client, or just bad timing. Women, on the other hand, tend to focus on their own role, on what *they* did wrong. Although such self-awareness can be beneficial, taking it to extremes or sharing insights with too many people can also diminish our talents and cost us in the long run.

Take Davis. She relayed doubts and setbacks in her work to her boss, unwittingly acting against herself. If that hasn't hurt her already, by causing the loss of her client, it will in the future, by providing her enemies with ammunition. Even those who aren't her foes will question her competence if she keeps telling them about every misstep she makes.

Davis condemns Singer for his boasting. He may well be a shameless self-promoter, but there is nothing wrong with strengthening your reputation. Davis has to try to put the best spin on her loss of the account. She should rehearse one tactful and credible explanation, then stick to it. If she feels the need to speak candidly, she should confide only in her closest, most trusted friends. The rest of her colleagues should hear her stock answer—and nothing else. She could talk about a new project that she is working on. A practiced shrug will help, along with a sense of humor. She should be careful about her body language and facial expressions as well. And she need not feel compelled to answer questions. The best way of deflecting unpleasant queries is by answering with a question of your own.

As for those private mistakes we all make, women need to

be more generous with themselves. Forgetting a client's name or slipping up on a report is embarrassing, but forgivable. Instead of collecting these small mistakes and then recounting them to friends and foes alike, get through the unpleasant moment, learn your lesson, and move on.

In the meantime, take comfort in knowing that many people have turned their worst failures into their biggest successes. Jenny Craig, Jean Nidetch, and Susan Powter have all built weight-control empires after years of fighting obesity. Incompatibility with her co-anchor led Barbara Walters to leave ABC News and resurface as a star interviewer on *20/20*. Even the archetypal optimist Dale Carnegie had to bounce back, starting his legendary speaking course, after having failed as a novelist and then eking out a living as a salesman for a trucking company in New York. All of these people used failure to build new careers or enhance old ones. Others can—and must—do the same.

Too Much to Do?
How to Take
Charge

Only dead-end jobs
are easy. Here's how to get
it all done when you
can't do it all.

Marva Lewis, an accountant at a metals manufacturer, is in over-drive. Initially she was thrilled to be given more responsibilities, especially that of overseeing the closing of the fiscal year. She recognized that her new duties would mean a lot more work but felt her prior experience in meeting monthly and quarterly dead-lines would help her ride out the rough transition.

But now her job is demanding more of her time than ever, and the needless interruptions and responsibilities are beginning to weigh on her. Handling taxes always brings pressures, but with the closing of the fiscal year she has also had to deal with a slew of independent accountants camped out in the conference room. And she is still responsible for the detail work that she's always had.

Now her boss, Jim McCormack, the assistant controller, has asked her to help him design visual aids for his next presentation before the stockholders. It's a good opportunity to get visibility and some insight into the big picture, but she knows it will mean even longer hours.

Lewis has always enjoyed working hard and under pressure, and she relishes her new duties. But now she is beginning to face the reality that she may not be able to handle all of her work. She wonders whether she should tell McCormack and demand relief. But what kind of relief? Should she give up her new duties, which she enjoys, duties which could prove valuable in her advancement?

GETTING HELP WHEN YOU'RE SWAMPED

With the closing of the fiscal year upon her, Marva Lewis already feels overworked. But she does not want to turn down her boss's request for help in designing visual aids for his presentation at the next stockholders' meetings. It is an opportunity for her to get some exposure and show off her talents. Rather than complaining or playing the role of silent martyr, Lewis informs her boss, Jim McCormack, of her situation and suggests solutions.

LEWIS: I guess I don't have to tell you what an incredibly hectic time of year we're in.

MCCORMACK: That's the understatement of the year! How is everything going with you? Are the accountants keeping you busy?

LEWIS: Well, that's what I wanted to talk to you about. You know, I've got a lot on my plate right now. I'm supervising the independent accountants, who are camped out in the conference room right now, and we're working around the clock to meet the April 15 deadline. And I'm wrapping up all the miscellaneous paperwork dealing with the end of the fiscal year.

MCCORMACK: As you said, this is a busy time of year. But from what I hear, you're doing a bang-up job.

LEWIS: Thank you. But I have to be frank. I'm very excited about working on the visual-aids presentation with you. It's a wonderful opportunity. But I'm concerned that I won't be able to give it all the attention it needs—and that I want to give to it.

MCCORMACK: Do you want me to find someone else to do it?

LEWIS: Oh, no. I think I could be of real assistance to you, and I really want to do it. I just need an assistant assigned to me temporarily to help draw up the charts for the presentation. I could do the conceptual thinking, and the assistant—maybe Jeannie Parks from operations would be available?—could put my ideas into chart form. That would save me an enormous amount of time and save you from having to break in someone new.

MCCORMACK: Marva, let me talk to Jeannie's supervisor and see if she would be free. Otherwise, we might be able to bring in a freelancer for two or three days. How does that sound?

LEWIS: Good. Thanks Jim.

STRATEGY

MARVA Lewis needs to make a move, but complaining to her boss is not it. A smart executive takes responsibility for assessing her own priorities and limits. When she has completed this assessment, she goes to her boss—not with anger and frustration, but with alternatives and possible solutions. Instead of feeling overwhelmed, Lewis should begin the long-term career strategy of learning to manage her workload.

We tend to think of a job's requirements as fixed and finite. But the fact is that every job involves a continuous learning process, requiring us to keep mastering new responsibilities and managing our workload and time. That is what leads to growth and promotions. The only jobs that are static are dead-end jobs. The sooner Lewis accepts this reality, the sooner she will stop expecting her boss to manage her job for her, and the faster and higher she will advance in her company.

The first thing she needs to do is identify what, given her limited time and resources, can and cannot be accomplished. I know the difficulties this task can pose. I am privy to the agonies of my upwardly moving clients; they, like Lewis, are frequently diligent, conscientious women who try to do too much. They're caught in the worker-bee syndrome (a syndrome that's much more common, incidentally, than the better-known queen-bee phenomenon). The worker bee holds on to old tasks that she knows she can perform well partly because she fears she won't be able to perform new tasks and partly because she doesn't like to say no. Nor does she want to admit that she can't do it all. The result is not a manager but a martyr. This can be disastrous: Not only does it unnecessarily burden the worker bee; it also sends a message to management that she cannot get on top of her job.

Lewis has not reached that point yet, but she still takes time for such tasks as reading and clipping articles from accounting journals and answering clients' routine questions, both of which could easily by done by her secretary. Those were duties and luxuries that she had time for when her job was smaller. Now she must relinquish the security of performing assigned tasks and take on the risk of new duties, even creating them for herself. By showing she can handle larger and more complex projects, she proves her worthiness for a bigger job.

Although Lewis does not have a staff to delegate tasks to, she does have a secretary. She needs to learn how to use her to streamline her day. She might, for instance, have her secretary draft form letters to handle certain client queries. She also might have her hold phone calls and take detailed messages so Lewis doesn't waste time on the phone.

What if Lewis assesses her job, enlists her secretary's help, and finds she still has too much to do? Then she will have a legitimate issue to discuss with McCormack. No boss is omniscient. McCormack may not have been aware of the heaviness of Lewis's workload when he asked for her help in designing visual aids for his next stockholders' presentation. But even so, that is no reason to allow the situation to persist.

As an employee and a professional, Lewis must not allow herself to try to do an undoable job. That's not good for her *or* the company. If the job is too big, she should suggest alternatives: hiring a temporary worker to help her in designing the visual aids or postponing another project.

During the next few years, many of us will face cutbacks in staff without lessened responsibilities. We might take that as an opportunity to steer our management in the direction of reassessment of expectations and accomplishments.

Since change is always a factor in our careers, we have to learn more than just how to cope with the phenomenon. We have to learn how to take charge of it. We should not settle for doing more with less when we have the opportunity to redefine our concepts of what we do and how we do it. In the process, we develop more than our jobs—we develop ourselves.

BUILDING
YOUR TOLERANCE
FOR RISK

> In a lean and mean era,
> those who play it safe may
> be the first ones
> out of work.

The memo announcing the merger came nearly six months ago, but Liz Brennan, a CPA at one of the world's largest accounting firms, is still in shock. The thirty-seven-year-old has worked for the same company since graduating from college fifteen years ago. Her responsibilities and salary have steadily increased over the years; she expected to be named a partner in a year or two and intended to spend the rest of her career at the firm.

Then the merger was announced. Like so many other accounting firms, Brennan's employer is joining forces with another to better compete in the world market. That means layoffs. No one knows when, or which departments will be hit, but most of Brennan's peers aren't waiting around to find out. They are circulating their résumés and politicking heavily, lunching with clients and partners, showing off their knowledge at meetings and churning out memos proposing new "cost-cutting" and "innovative" programs.

Brennan knows she should do the same, but she has never been good at pushing herself. She works hard but never does more than is required. In fact, she entered accounting precisely because she knew job security would be virtually guaranteed if she were competent and loyal. Brennan held up her end of the bargain, but just when she was supposed to reap the benefits, the rules changed.

Not only has her firm merged with another, but the entire industry has undergone a transformation in recent years. Because of other mergers and acquisitions, the Big Eight—a group made up of the world's largest and formerly most stable accounting companies—has shrunk to the Big Six. No one is secure anymore; even partners are being fired.

"Don't worry," counseled her brother, a Wall Street dynamo who has survived many upheavals. "Volunteer to give the next presentation and come up with a plan that dazzles your bosses. Then they'll keep you around." Easy for him, Brennan thinks. Her brother thrives on risk; he is willing to lose a lot to win even more. She isn't. All she wants is a secure position in a stable company.

□ TESTING THE WATERS: □ SEVEN STEPS

No one can count on job security in today's volatile economy. Only the most productive employees can avoid being laid off, and even then there's no guarantee. That means all managers must increase their tolerance for risk. While some risk takers seem to have a natural propensity for it, others can develop a taste. Here's how.

1. *Assess the possible outcomes of all your options.* Ask yourself which alternative offers you the most loss or gain. Which scenario do you dread the most?

2. *Start small.* At the next question-and-answer period of a conference, stand up, introduce yourself, compliment the speakers, then ask a question or make a comment. Initiate informal conversations with your boss or your boss's boss; discuss some of your ideas with colleagues. As with any skill, risk taking requires practice.

3. *Join a professional association, a Toastmasters club, or a volunteer organization requiring you to make speeches.* That will help you overcome your fear of standing apart from the crowd.

4. *Stretch the boundaries of what you consider safe.* Enroll in an Outward Bound event, an acting class, or a foreign-language seminar.

5. *If you want to take action but your anxieties are holding you back, pretend that you are one of your most aggressive co-workers.* What would he or she do in your shoes?

6. *Make a big splash by unveiling an ambitious plan or offering a big idea at a meeting of upper management.*

7. *Flood your bosses with ideas.* Even if some of them are rejected or are flops, you will gain attention and win respect for having confidence and creativity.

STRATEGY

EVERY accomplishment—from getting a promotion to launching a new business—requires taking leaps into the unknown. Some people, often society's greatest achievers, take risks eagerly;

they relish them, understanding that there's a chance they might fail but fueled by the fervent belief that they might succeed.

But many, like Brennan, dread uncertainty. Having been raised by families in which they were assured that one day would be just like the next, they try to re-create the stability and complete security they enjoyed (or wish they had enjoyed) as children.

In the past, even the most risk-averse people could lead successful careers. They could hide out in large corporations or the civil service, diligently doing their jobs, working their way up the corporate hierarchy, never innovating but never offending, and in the end they would be rewarded with a good salary and secure employment. That is obviously what Brennan had in mind when she chose accounting in the mid-1970s.

But as Brennan has discovered, corporate America has changed radically. Companies are making severe cutbacks in staffing and spending, and job security is a luxury afforded to few. Heads of corporations are routinely deposed for not improving productivity. In this lean and mean era, those who avoid risks are often the first to find themselves out of work. Employees must constantly prove their value; loyalty and seniority will not protect them any longer.

Today, everyone—not just the ambitious types like Brennan's brother—must build a tolerance for risk. Although I agree that some people may have a natural propensity for risk taking, I know that those who don't can learn this skill. First, you must identify and assess the risk at hand, weighing the possible gains against the potential losses for each course of action you could take. You try to pinpoint the scenario that would benefit you the most.

In Brennan's case, her immediate fear was losing her job. She has two basic options: She can fight for her job—a fight that may or may not prove successful—or she can continue to do nothing, which almost certainly will lead to her dismissal, given the company's situation. In short, she has a lot more to gain by trying.

Once Brennan realizes that, she should begin her campaign for her job, but she should take small steps. As with any skill, handling risk takes practice and confidence. If she were learning to ice-skate, she wouldn't perform for a panel of judges her first time out on the ice. Just so, she shouldn't begin with a presentation before her bosses, as her brother suggests. Instead, she should make a conscious effort to be more visible at meetings, asking questions and offering opinions.

At the same time, she needs to convince top management that she is essential. She should follow her peers' examples and write memos and plans, offering her ideas. The more she can put forward, the better, to show her can-do spirit, the kind of manager needed in tough times. She can start by researching how other accounting firms have handled mergers. She may discover certain areas of expertise that become essential during restructurings; making herself knowledgeable in those areas will minimize her chances of being laid off. At the least, she might find strategies other accounting firms have employed that her firm could borrow. She can then share her ideas with supervisors and colleagues. Not only will she be advertising her knowledge, she'll also be transforming herself from being afraid to being positive, confident, and forward-thinking.

If she has trouble mustering the courage to take action, she should remind herself of her cocky colleagues who consistently make such bold moves even though they are no smarter than she is. If she could imagine that she is one of them, she has only to do what they would do. What Brennan doesn't understand is that those who often dare to voice their plans and opinions are usually appreciated more, even if some of their proposals are losers. Think about all the "ideas people" you know of (many of them probably men) who have been promoted or praised despite the fact that some of their projects bombed. Like athletes or studio executives, you'll be remembered even if only a few of your attempts are big hits.

Some of Brennan's suggestions might fail or be rejected, but she, too, will gain from the exposure. In fact, visibility, rather than being "right," is so important that I encourage clients to try to make a big splash, once they've gotten some practice under their belts. At a key meeting of top managers, in which they are welcoming bold new ideas, impress them with a wildly innovative plan. I remember hearing about one young woman, for instance, who was invited to listen in on a major brainstorming meeting of the senior staff at her company. Instead of just fading into the background, she put forward an ambitious proposal. Though it was rejected as too costly to execute, the gesture put her on the map as a thinker. Subsequently, her opinions were often solicited—and well respected. She received more challenging projects and greater rewards.

Similarly, Brennan needs to force herself to take risks. She will never be like her brother who enjoys the danger involved, but with practice, she can—and must—make herself into a moderate risk taker. In this economic climate, avoiding risk is taking the biggest risk of all.

SMARTER DECISION MAKING

> No matter how skilled
> you are, your career will
> suffer if you can't
> make choices.

Marianne Stein's boss cornered her after the staff meeting and delivered a polite but unmistakable warning: "Make a decision by Friday." Stein, an account supervisor in charge of accessories at a mail-order company, was to recommend whether or not to include a new vendor's merchandise in the summer catalog. But at the meeting, Stein had demurred, saying she was waiting for a market-research report.

But she was stalling. For weeks she has been unable to make up her mind. She likes the product line but worries that in this economy it might not sell, the last thing her ailing company needs. However, if she rejects the merchandise and it becomes a hot item elsewhere, wouldn't that hurt her reputation? Her boss, Lou Donaldson, vice president of marketing, has already told her that he thinks she is overly cautious. Should she be super-aggressive to prove him wrong?

Stein has always gone through this kind of mental gymnastics before making a decision, but lately she has been waffling as she has more decision-making responsibilities. Even when Stein does resolve an issue, she wallows in self-doubt afterward, wondering what would have happened had she made a different choice. And when she errs, she castigates herself—or her staff—mercilessly. Why didn't they give her the information she needed? Why didn't she ask for it? The fact that her instincts have often proved correct hasn't boosted her self-confidence. At those times, Stein tells herself she was lucky—she could make a terrible mistake.

Thursday night, after reviewing the new merchandise for hours, Stein watches the clock turn to three a.m. She is still worried. Won't Donaldson lose faith in her is she doesn't give a smart recommendation? But how can she force herself to decide?

☐
DECIDING TO DECIDE: 10 QUESTIONS TO EASE THE TASK
☐

Many managers find decision making difficult. They are smart and diligent, but when it comes to settling on a course of action, they resort to delaying tactics, or they blame others to duck responsibility. Below are ten questions to ask yourself in order to help you overcome your block.

1. Do I have to make this decision alone?
2. What is the basic issue that I must address and resolve?
3. Do I have all (or enough) of the information I need?
4. Whom, inside or outside my firm, can I consult?
5. How have I handled similar issues in the past? Would I do anything differently?
6. Do I have a track record of making poor decisions? If so, why? Can I change?

7. Do I rely too heavily—or not heavily enough—on experts' opinions?
8. If the stakes appear too high, is there a compromise that I can settle on as a safety net?
9. Whose style of decision making do I admire, and why?
10. If I were to set my alarm clock to ring in ten minutes, what would my decision then be?

STRATEGY

STEIN is right to be concerned. She is obviously intelligent and conscientious, but unless she can overcome her fear of decision making, her career will stall. For few bosses will trust someone who doesn't have the confidence to trust herself—and self-confidence is ultimately what decision making requires.

Stein's problem is not unusual. I've noticed that women tend to assume that they don't know enough, whereas men, generally speaking, believe they do. Furthermore, a woman is likely to say that her good decisions are due to luck and her bad ones to incompetence, while a man is apt to dismiss his failures as bad luck and credit his successes to his talents. The result is that men feel confident enough to make choices, while women fear failing and being "found out," so they avoid making the final call.

I don't mean to imply that men always resolve work issues successfully. In fact, some, in their zeal to be decisive, leap to the wrong conclusions. But at work, you aren't penalized nearly as harshly for making a poor decision as for not making any decision at all. Think about it: When a referee makes a call that directly opposes the crowd's view, he is neither disregarded nor fired. Occasional arbitrariness is accepted as part of the game.

Stein needs to learn this lesson. If her recommendation is

well founded but isn't borne out for some reason, her boss isn't likely to blame her. But avoiding her responsibility and failing to make a deadline are cardinal sins that few managers can stand.

For Stein to conquer her fear of decision making, she needs to look at herself objectively. Does she have a history of making poor choices? If so, can she recognize an underlying pattern? For instance, does she ignore the advice of experts—or trust them too much? In Stein's case, I would guess she probably has a fairly good track record; otherwise she wouldn't have the authority that she has now.

Stein then must look at the winning choices she has made. Did she stumble upon the answers, or did they come after research and deliberation? If she tallied the results, comparing her success rate when she relied on others with her rate when she trusted her instincts, then she would have real data so that she could reframe her internal thinking from "I've been lucky" to "I've been smart."

As for Stein's immediate problem, she needs to concentrate on the essential questions. It is not whether she is risk-averse (though that bears examining at another time). What she needs to resolve now is whether to include the new merchandise. Stein must not confuse the issue (or herself) by obsessing over ancillary questions; she must remain focused on the problem.

Before she can make any recommendations, however, she must make sure she has analyzed the product line thoroughly. Research is the basis for any sound decision. Stein is right to try to secure marketing projections (although she shouldn't have used it as a delaying tactic). But she could also consult others, both inside and outside the firm, who have resolved similar issues. Or she can ask colleagues and employees for their input: What do they think are the questions she needs to consider?

Research alone, however, is not a panacea. Many people who procrastinate rely on information too much, thinking that it will yield the single "right" answer. That is rarely the case. Most of the time the answer isn't clear-cut. Instead, it is up to the manager to forecast and weigh potential gains against possible losses. Which would be worse: losing out on a profitable product line or committing to a losing one?

Stein might try a compromise. She can hedge her bets and build in a safety net, perhaps by ordering the most promising half of the inventory. If she still feels at a loss, she could ask herself what she would recommend if she had to deliver her report in ten minutes. She might discover that she already knows the answer but lacks the confidence to act on it.

Ultimately, though, Stein may have to hazard a guess. If so, she should take comfort in the fact that it is an educated one, even if it comes with no guarantees. After all, managing requires taking responsible risks, which leads to greater rewards.

ARE YOU STRESSED
TO THE LIMIT?

At work and at home,
you're under pressure. You can't
get rid of the workload or cure
the economy, but you can
learn to cope.

The meeting took place three days ago, but Catherine Medwin, a sales manager at a large retail chain, is still upset. Though Medwin's boss, Donald Eng, and her co-worker, Bob Brown, were smiling and telling jokes, it seemed that they had arranged the supposedly impromptu get-together for the sole purpose of criticizing her. "You've got to learn to roll with the punches," Eng said. "Yeah, lighten up a little," Brown chimed in. "You're so uptight, you're even making *me* nervous."

Medwin said nothing at the time; she was too stunned to speak. She knows that she has been short-tempered and high-strung lately, but in her situation who wouldn't be? She has a new computer system to learn, a workload that grows daily, and employees in desperate need of a support staff that she can't afford to hire, not to mention a toddler who leaves a mess wherever he goes and a husband who refuses to pick up even after himself.

Eng's and Brown's comments only added to her worries.

What if her staff hears about the meeting? As it is, they don't exactly see her as a model manager. Two months ago, her over-worked, underpaid assistant sales managers asked for clerical help, saying they were so busy faxing and typing that they couldn't meet their deadlines. Medwin had to tell them that the company, having just made layoffs, would not make any new hires this year. To help out, Medwin has been taking on some of their work, leaving her little time to learn the new DOS system and to coordinate the projects she inherited from one of the laid-off managers.

Eng and Brown were sympathetic to Medwin's plight—"We know you're going through a rough period," Eng said—but their concern increased Medwin's fears. Would her job be on the line if she did not "lighten up"? If she lost her job, it could take her a year before she found another at her salary.

Medwin would love to be able to follow their advice; she wants nothing more than to put her worries behind her. But even when Medwin's life was running smoothly, she wasn't an easy-going person. Now that she is being pressured from all sides, how can she make herself carefree? Tucking her son into bed, she hopes that she won't spend another sleepless night.

FIVE SIMPLE WAYS TO
TEMPER THE TENSION

No one can escape stress, but you can learn to cope with it. Here's how.

1. *Seize control in small ways.* Take time to instill order wherever you can. Straighten up your desk. Clean out your Rolodex. Get rid of unnecessary clutter.

2. *Practice positive thinking.* It may sound corny, but it pays to remind yourself of your successes—frequently. Re-

hearse a few uplifting sound bites, such as, "I made partner because I do good work." Repeat them to yourself to prevent drowning in negativity.

3. *Stop worrying.* Whenever you begin to fret about hypothetical situations or "what-if" scenarios, take a simple test: Rank the events that are bothering you in order of severity and assess their probability of happening. Review the list a month later for a reality check. Soon you will become adept at seeing these worries for what they are—imaginary.

4. *Prioritize.* Don't do it all; don't even try. Make the household tasks a shared responsibility for you and your mate or hire a cleaning service, and delegate what you can at work.

5. *Pamper yourself.* Unrelieved stress can result in serious health problems. Learn what relaxes you—whether it's dancing or massages—and make time for it.

☐   ☐

STRATEGY

STRESS is an inescapable part of modern life. Technologies such as fax machines and computers provide a constant stream of information to be immediately processed and new systems to be mastered. More recently, people have also had to deal with a poor economy in which workloads are doubled, raises are puny, and job security no longer exists. In a 1992 study by Northwestern National Life Insurance, 46 percent of the participants said their jobs were highly stressful—more than double the number who said so in a 1985 U.S. Department of Health and Human Services survey. Only 4 percent of the 1,299 respondents said they were nearly stress-free; 39 percent were thinking of quitting their jobs because of work-related stress.

From what I have seen, women are particularly hard hit by stress. Not only do they face pressure at work, but they also struggle with it at home. In her 1989 book *The Second Shift*, sociologist Arlie Hochschild detailed the working mother's plight: After working a full day at the office, she often puts in a full shift a home. In fact, Hochschild calculated, women work an average of fifteen hours a week more than their husbands do. As a result, many women are angry, frustrated, and anxious.

So Medwin isn't alone. The question is, what can she do about it? First, she needs to understand the underlying cause of stress. Whether it comes in the form of information overload, economic pressures, or overwork, stress is the result of feeling a lack of control. Medwin feels overwhelmed as if she is a victim. What she needs to do, then, is empower herself.

She might begin with small, obvious steps. She could take an hour to clean off her desk and remove the clutter that makes her feel constantly behind and overwhelmed. She could also keep prioritized lists of what she needs to do, allocating the time she will devote to each task and forcing herself to stick to it. One of my clients set a timer so that she would never spend more than thirty minutes at a staff meeting. Medwin should do whatever she can think of to instill order in her life.

Medwin also needs to prioritize responsibilities. What must she do, what can she ignore, and what should she delegate? From what I've observed, much stress is at least partly self-induced, the result of unrealistic expectations. That is certainly the case with Medwin. She wants to do her work, her employees' work, and the housework. Like a lot of women, she is trying to do it all— and she can't. She must relieve herself of whatever duties she can and focus on what's most important.

That means persuading her husband to do his fair share at home. Many women resent their double shift, but they are afraid to challenge it because, unconsciously, they believe it is their wifely duty (and, unfortunately, so do their husbands). Unless Medwin and her husband can afford to hire household help, though, they will have to overcome these stereotypes.

Similarly, while it is admirable of Medwin to share her employees' work, it isn't wise, given her own daunting workload. Since Eng has expressed his concern for her, Medwin might explain the situation and request a temporary aide. If he can't provide one, then Medwin must ask her staff to be patient until the situation changes. She should make sure to show her appreciation for their efforts. Even a handwritten thank-you note can make a difference.

Medwin also needs to be kind to herself. She expects to excel at everything and punishes herself for failing to do so. Here is an irony: Often, the more pressured people feel, the more they add to the problem with self-criticism. Medwin needs to keep her perspective: to differentiate between the crisis and the irritant. Is her inability to use the new system right now a tragedy? And while it is unfortunate that she can't get extra help in for her staff, they will survive being temporarily overworked, and so will she.

Equally important, Medwin must stop fretting about hypothetical situations. She is tormenting herself with "what-ifs," such as whether her staff might learn about the meeting and what she would do if Eng fired her. Both dilemmas are possible, but are they likely?

Instead of focusing on the bleakest pictures, Medwin might begin to look at the bright side. She could have interpreted Eng's and Brown's comments as gestures of support rather than condescension. The more Medwin concentrates on the positive, the more likely it is that she will feel optimistic.

So far, Medwin is relatively lucky—all she has experienced is a few sleepless nights. For many people, stress results in serious medical problems, ranging from migraines to heart attacks. The National Council on Compensation Insurance says the average stress-related workers' compensation claim costs employers at least

$13,339, leading many companies to expand their employee-assistance programs and wellness programs to include sessions on stress management.

Medwin may protest that she doesn't have the time or energy to do all that I suggest. But she should keep in mind that stress is not a one-time occurrence. Once Medwin makes these changes, she will find that she copes better with the many new pressures she will surely face in the future.

COPING WITH AGEISM

In today's economy it's not only the over-fifty crowd that has to worry about discrimination.

Anne Lever never imagined that she would find herself in this situation. For seventeen years, Lever has been an advertising sales executive for an international magazine publishing company, and for most of that time she has been a top performer, consistently winning awards for exceeding sales quotas. Now, at forty-eight, just when she thought she would be reaping the benefits of her years of hard work and enjoying a solid reputation, she finds herself being ignored by her thirty-two-year-old boss, Bob Williams, the vice president of sales, and her co-workers, most of whom are some twenty years younger than she is.

For months Lever has been offering to make presentations at the weekly staff meetings, but to no avail. Williams always says "Great!" but then conveniently forgets to make time for them. She resents his disregard for her knowledge and thinks he could benefit from the experience she has in ad sales, often from dealing with executives more talented then he is. She can't remember the last time anyone thought to invite her to lunch or even asked her for advice. Lever believes her co-workers are immature and arrogant know-it-alls who assume that she, being over forty, must be "out of it" or "senile" (put-downs her colleagues have used to describe competitors her age).

"That's age discrimination," a friend said when she related her story. But the truth is, as unhappy as she is with her situation, Lever understands the human desire to want to work with people the same age. After all, you like the same music, you wear the same clothes, and you're inspired by the same things. For example, the prizes and games Williams uses to encourage the sales executives—like taking the whole staff to dinner at a four-star restaurant, followed by dancing at a chic club—work well to motivate her peers, but she finds them uninviting. At this point in her life, she would rather get home and go to bed at a decent hour than stay out late with her co-workers.

With her twenty-fifth anniversary at the company only a month away, Lever wonders: Should she quit and find work with a more mature group?

STRATEGY

SOMEHOW, most of us never expect to be among the oldest in the crowd, but, of course, it happens. And when it happens in the workplace, it does have devastating effects, as Lever has learned. When the sixties dictum "Never trust anyone over thirty" has gone the way of love beads and flower power, stereotypes still abound about older people.

Dunhill Personnel System, an international employment-service organization, recently surveyed 266 workers twenty-five to thirty-five years old; the respondents believed younger workers (those twenty-five to thirty-five) are more motivated, flexible, and independent as well as better educated than workers forty-five and older. Companies frequently target older workers for layoffs during hard times. The Conference Board, a nonprofit group that studies business issues, reported that 40 percent of the 406 major corporations it surveyed in 1992 said they were offering early-retirement packages. Corporations are interested in cutting costs—older workers tend to be higher paid—and no one doubts that the companies are making room for more "cost-efficient" employees: younger workers who, they believe, work more aggressively, faster, and smarter as well as for less money. Worse, in this tough, cost-cutting environment, the age at which you can be considered over the hill seems to be dropping. I'm hearing more and more stories about women in their late thirties being replaced by women in their late twenties.

Still, Lever's first response to ageism on the job shouldn't be to quit. Based on 1992 figures, U.S. Bureau of Labor statistics estimate that 4.6 million management jobs are held by people under the age of thirty-five, so it is unlikely that she will be able to avoid working with younger people. Instead, she needs to combat their prejudice and bridge the so-called generation gap.

She can start by focusing on the present. Like many veteran employees, Lever wants her record to speak for itself. But it doesn't. No one remembers what she did in the early eighties. What counts is what she is doing today. So, what is she doing now? Upset that they don't appreciate her, Lever has been hiding and finding reasons why she can't get along with her colleagues.

Ironically, she has been focusing on the age difference just as much as she accuses her co-workers of doing. Instead of minimizing the gap, she obsesses about differences in attitude, dress, and musical taste. She has even been spouting a few of her own stereotypes, calling her associates "immature" and "arrogant." Lever needs to put aside her hurt feelings and become her own champion.

How can she do that? First, she should share her knowledge and become a mentor to some of the staff. Instead of harping on her co-workers' ages, she needs to see them as individuals and find at least one with whom she might develop a rapport. There must be someone whom she admires or who reminds her of herself, or who she wanted to be at that age? Rather than waiting for an invitation to lunch, she should take the lead and arrange a date. When she sees others struggling with a project, she should offer her friendly input and avoid condescending comments like "Believe me, I know how it's done."

While Lever doesn't have to start dressing like an MTV clone, she does need to show that she is not out of it. Projecting vitality and maintaining good health and fitness habits are important. And keeping current with trends in her field is essential; job descriptions are changing dramatically and rapidly because of technological advances. Understandably, many older managers who weren't raised with computers are reluctant to join the technological revolution. But to be competitive and keep your current job, you must constantly learn. According to the American Association of Retired Persons, half of what you need to know today to keep your job will probably be obsolete by the year 2000. Lever must leave herself open to progress and change. She should keep up-to-date by taking courses, attending industry seminars, and plugging into the in-house expertise all around her.

All these actions may also help her win over her younger boss. But she needs to meet with him to ask exactly how she can make herself more valuable to the organization. My guess is that he feels patronized by her. Lever needs to demonstrate that she respects him and is willing to earn his respect and contribute to the bottom line. Rather than comparing him to her predecessors, she should acknowledge the traits she admires in him and receive his observations and recommendations willingly and with an open mind. By doing so, she will also show that she perceives him as her supervisor rather than as a thirty-two-year-old upstart.

What if all this fails and the age discrimination continues? To protect herself, she might begin keeping a record of the work she does and the comments it elicits. But given that a lawsuit is time-consuming, emotionally draining, alienating to future employers, and tough to win, suing should be a last resort.

With baby-boomers now approaching fifty, many of the myths about aging may be dispelled: the cult of youth might even lose some of its appeal. (Already, boomer authors are destig-matizing menopause.) Until then, though, it's up to individuals to prove by example that a person's ability to get the job done *doesn't* decline with age.

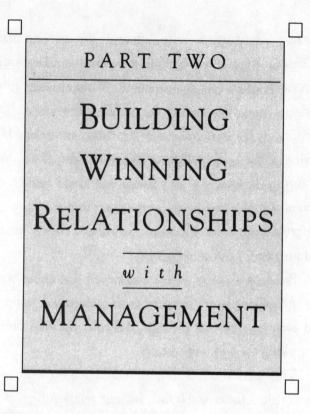

PART TWO

BUILDING WINNING RELATIONSHIPS

with

MANAGEMENT

 ho could have known that our bosses would turn out to be so different from our teachers? In school, we carefully learned to recite back what was asked for on tests and papers, waited for our good grades, and then were automatically promoted. Protected by our teachers, we learned an unwritten and detrimental lesson: to depend on the system.

In real life, few of us are fired because we have failed to do a good job, even though too many of us live with this fear. The truth is quite different: We lose out mainly because we have failed to build a supportive relationship with our bosses—our management. Without clear role models or mentors, we mistake building that critical relationship for manipulative politicking, an updated version of the apple polishing of school days. If we do, we turn aside from the very bonds that could launch our careers and provide our greatest opportunities. Unfortunately, most opportunities are not clearly labeled and are often hard to recognize.

Building a career means more than just doing your job and getting by: It requires us to understand, support, and even nurture that tenuous, difficult, yet vital process of working for and with others.

This section offers insight and advice on some of the most critical issues you'll face in your relationships at work—and how to make the most of them.

YOUR BOSS
JUST STOLE YOUR IDEA:
CAN YOU GET IT BACK?

> When you have created
> a concept, you need to claim
> it and any rewards.

Margaret Green, an account executive at a midsize ad agency, was livid as she put down the phone. Her client Ned Silver had praised the marketing strategy she'd designed for Dairy Foods, but he'd given all the credit to the account supervisor—her boss, George Hammer. "Hammer is a real visionary," Silver had said. "You can learn a lot from him."

For Green that was the last straw. She'd worked late every night last week outlining a revolutionary campaign to revive Dairy Foods' sluggish market share. At first Hammer resisted the radical concept she'd described in her memo, but she convinced him that it would put Dairy Foods back on the map. He pumped her for details before he joined Silver and the management supervisor, Bill Meyer, in a closed-door meeting.

Green assumed that Hammer would credit her with the brainchild she'd worked so hard to develop. But the conversation with her client has convinced her that he presented her ground-breaking proposal as his own. And only this morning she over-heard Meyer praising Hammer's "state-of-the-art thinking."

It isn't the first time this kind of thing has happened. For several months Green has felt that she's carried the Dairy Foods account with little input from Hammer. She's made copies of all the memos she's sent him. Now she's considering spilling the story to Meyer with an ultimatum: "Hammer goes or I do."

STRATEGY

GREEN is justifiably enraged, but demanding a showdown will only place her in jeopardy. Savvy as she is about her account, she's naive about how things work at the top. Nothing she can claim, short of murder, will motivate Meyer to fire Hammer—especially not now, when he's in the client's good graces.

Green needs to be warned that men at the top stick together and are slow to make any changes among themselves. Besides, demanding ownership of the idea *after* it has proved successful only makes her sound like a poor sport. If Green confronts Hammer, all she'll gain is an enemy. Sure, she's got the documentation to prove her story, but winning this battle may cause her to lose the war.

There's a reason the law doesn't copyright ideas: It's nearly impossible to prove who really did the ground breaking and who expanded the concept. It's Green's job to come up with good ideas, just as it's Hammer's job to recognize them. He may have even modified the idea somewhat before presenting it. Hammer no doubt feels completely justified in "borrowing" the concept.

Green is lucky in some respects. After all, Hammer has given her the opportunity to think for herself about high-level problems. Besides, since Hammer represents the whole account team, upper management probably already assumes Green has had a hand in devising the proposal—that's what they pay her to do! Yet Green is trapped in a corporate system where ideas and information are handed up by employees who have no direct way of getting credit for what they do.

What angers Green is that Hammer didn't come through for her and toot her horn to the big boss. Sounds great, but she should have learned long ago that he isn't the kind of manager who grooms his subordinates for bigger things.

So far Green's biggest mistake has been to ignore the importance of forging links with top management. Even the most hierarchical corporations offer some access to people at the top, at least on a casual basis. Had Green brought herself into the inner circle before this time, she might have asked Meyer for advice about Hammer or let him know how discouraged she is, despite her wish to stay on. In fact, she even might have dropped a comment that let him know she was responsible for the brainstorm.

Since Green has not taken measures to protect herself, she has no choice but to let this idea go. Now's the time, however, to plant the seeds that may prevent this kind of thing from happening again.

What should she ask for? An invitation to be included in those top-level meetings. Not only will that mean validation and acceptance by the firm's movers and shakers, but it will provide her with the opportunity to present her own ideas. People will figure out quickly that she's the brains behind the operation.

But Hammer is not going to offer Green this entrée unless she asks for it. Even then it's going to take some luck for her to get her way. Green can shift the odds in her favor by using some smart negotiation tools (see box).

If Hammer blocks her request, Green will have to take more aggressive action (send Meyer copies of all future memos, for instance). But whatever happens, Hammer will know that Green is bucking to be recognized.

NEGOTIATING TO GET IN WHERE YOU BELONG

Hammer respects Green's intelligence; otherwise he wouldn't "borrow" her ideas. She should use that respect as leverage. Green has another advantage: Hammer needs her. Here's what she should say.

GREEN (*casually*): George, I'm so glad Ned backed our idea—I knew it was going to be a winning strategy.

HAMMER (*generously*): Yeah, we couldn't have done it without you.

GREEN: Part of the reason our department works is that everyone feels comfortable sharing ideas with the team.

HAMMER: Absolutely.

GREEN: You always push us to give the best possible product to the client.

HAMMER: Of course.

GREEN (*smiles*): Well, I have an idea that will help us deliver even better service in the future.

HAMMER (*laughs*): Okay, what are you asking for?

GREEN: I'd like the opportunity to participate in the big client meetings.

HAMMER (*frowning*): I don't know; they're usually just for department heads.

GREEN: I know that's usually the case, but with this particular client I've taken a much more active role. It might be helpful to Silver for me to be there on the firing line, since I work with him on a daily basis. And it would help us sell the concept because I have all the back-up information to support our pitch.

HAMMER: Well . . .

GREEN: You know he always asks all those picky questions.

HAMMER: That's for sure . . . Look, it's really up to Bill Meyer whether you come in or not.

GREEN: How about if I come with you when you hit him with this? (*Hammer pauses.*) I can do that tomorrow morning at ten-thirty; is that a good time for you? George, I can't tell you how much this means to me.

HAMMER: Let me check my schedule.

☐   ☐

Green has been careful to allow Hammer to save face; unconsciously he's grateful for that, and this helps her negotiation proceed favorably. By getting him to say yes to a few general observations, she's made him receptive to the more important conversation that follows. She also has pitched her suggestion as a way to give the client better service—something that interests both of them. Finally, she has pinned him down by asking him to set an exact meeting time.

Same Job, New Boss: Can You Make It Work?

> Since situations don't come nicely labeled, we have to treat some obstacles as if they were opportunities.

Laura Gelson is worried. Her boss and mentor, Betsy Hart, resigned a few weeks ago, and she's just met Hart's replacement, Brad Schmidt. With one look at Schmidt's conservative suit and stiff demeanor, Gelson could tell that he and Hart have very different working styles. Now she's concerned that Schmidt's arrival will throw a wrench in her fast-moving career as products manager for a multinational corporation.

The department had thrived under Hart and turned a 27 percent profit last year from three newly launched products. But Gelson knows that Hart's entrepreneurial spirit caused her to butt heads with the president occasionally, and she's not surprised that Hart left to run a small manufacturing start-up.

Now Gelson has to face Schmidt, who headed up the manufacturing division of a competing corporation. He's reputed to be smart, though a company man. Gelson loves her job and is committed to the company. But she's concerned about playing number two to a different leader. Does she have a shot with Schmidt?

STRATEGY

GETTING a new boss—especially when you're in the upper ranks—never can be taken lightly. Although Gelson doesn't have to deal with the "guilt by association" she'd confront if her former mentor had been dismissed, her concern is warranted. Old players often are ousted to make way for new blood. For an enlightened and lucky few, however, a new boss offers opportunity. And since situations don't come nicely labeled, we have to treat some obstacles as if they were opportunities. They might be.

Gelson should resist the temptation to send out her résumé, answer ads, or call headhunters. Her actions may backfire and, in the worst case, force her into an untimely exit. Certainly they'll pull her off-course by steering her away from her job.

Instead, she should delve deeper and find out more about Schmidt's management style, decision-making ability, and track record, with both newly acquired staff and, of course, women managers.

Gelson probably has a two- or three-month safety net, since most new managers take at least that long before making any significant changes in policy or staff. But she should begin immediately to position herself as a valuable asset (see box). Her goal during her first few meetings with Schmidt is to establish common bonds, demonstrate clear loyalty to him and the company, and show off her management skills. This is not the time for modesty.

Gelson's research will help her find out what she and Schmidt have in common—possibly an alma mater, vacation spot, or hobby. In fact, she should keep investigating until she finds that bond. Bonding and the trust it engenders become increasingly important as one moves into the upper ranks of management.

If Gelson doesn't take a shine to Schmidt, she's got to honestly evaluate her feelings and decide whether it's her new boss she dislikes or the change itself. Change is something most of us resist, especially when the change is not something we've helped to implement. To succeed now, Gelson's got to buy into Schmidt's modus operandi. Incorporating his ideas and putting them into practice not only demonstrates her loyalty to him but also her ability to be both creative and flexible. Schmidt's approach is different, but there's still a chance that he and Gelson will hit it off. In any case, Gelson must reject the feeling that she's selling out or kowtowing.

To shake that fallacy, Gelson might think of another model: the re-formed family. It's easy to understand the futility of a daughter's hating her new stepfather while continuing to revere her father, when she could have both relationships. Just so, Gelson needs to give Schmidt a genuine chance. All newly managed departments must undergo radical shifts of heart and habit. But good team players can learn to get along with almost any kind of boss.

To do this, Gelson must think like the professional she is and decide how she can best serve the organization and her new boss, as well as herself. She needs, for instance, to act as a guide and role model for her staff through this transition. An exodus of her own staffers won't help her.

Still, Gelson has to devise a plan B in case none of her efforts work. What are the warning signs? She's in trouble if Schmidt ignores her, makes condescending remarks in group meetings, doesn't invite her to meetings she used to go to, or bypasses her and talks directly to her staff. An early tip-off: In the first meetings Schmidt grows increasingly interested in how long she's been with the department, what her career goals are, and where she'd like to go next (emphasizing *go*). And if Schmidt immediately brings in his own people—especially if they're at or near Gelson's level—it's a signal that she's out.

Gelson soon will know whether Schmidt is getting rid of her, and whether she can work with him. If she can't, she should turn to her professional network (Hart included) for leads on other positions. True, Gelson shouldn't jump the gun. On the other hand, she shouldn't stick around until she's under fire.

REAL WORDS FOR REPOSITIONING

For Gelson it won't be enough to prove she does her job well technically; she has to start building a relationship with Schmidt. Many men, especially those of the old school, say they still feel uncomfortable with women executives. They feel awkward even when appropriately turning discourse from small talk to important business talk. So Gelson must steer the conversation. She shouldn't come in with both guns loaded, though. This calls for a subtler approach.

GELSON: How are you settling in? A little trial by fire, huh?

SCHMIDT: Nothing like pulling all-nighters your first week.

GELSON: Kind of pumps up your adrenaline, though. It reminds me of when we had to do group projects in B-school.

SCHMIDT: You're a Wharton grad, right?

GELSON: Class of '79.

SCHMIDT: Really? I taught a seminar there from '82 to '84. The campus has really changed. Have you been back?

GELSON: Last fall I gave a lecture on the new technology we launched that reduces bacteria. It was a task force on business's responsibility to the environment.

SCHMIDT: Oh, that's right, the company got some good PR from that.

GELSON: Yes, I was really glad it worked out. That project was sort of my baby. After seeing the response of the seminar, I got Betsy Hart to push the production date forward so we could get a jump on the market. We lucked out—G&B came out with their launch just two months later.

SCHMIDT: Right. Smart thinking. So what's your next brainchild?

GELSON: Well, that depends on you. What do you envision us focusing on?

Through her research Gelson found that she and Schmidt do indeed have a common bond: They both spent time at the same business school. She found an opening where she could drop the information naturally. Having established that link, she carefully steered the conversation to a more important matter—her performance. Then she turned the focus back to him to find out more about his vision. By doing this, she has demonstrated her openness to his ideas and, with luck, will find out whether his plans include her. Then she can decide on her long-term strategy.

PROMISES, PROMISES: CAN YOU MAKE YOUR BOSS DELIVER?

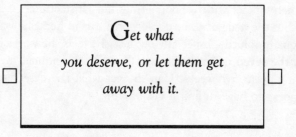

G*et what*
you deserve, or let them get
away with it.

When Nina Rockland took over the tax department as director last year, she was thrilled with the opportunity, even though she was told she'd have to prove herself before she would officially be given a vice president's title and the commensurate salary. But it's been a year now, and all Rockland's gotten is more work. She feels just about ready to quit.

Rockland, a CPA, is a tax specialist for one of the country's top five multinational textile corporations. She came to the company after graduating from college twelve years ago and has been steadily promoted ever since. Four months ago, another director (and a VP), Ron McHugh, suddenly quit, and Rockland was asked to manage his department as well as her own. She was given an extra assistant and a salary increase of 10 percent.

Rockland took the opportunity, but after a few inquiries she discovered that even with the raise, she's still making only two-thirds the former director's salary, and she still doesn't have the title.

Rockland reports to the CFO and senior vice president, Ken Perrone. He's brilliant and moderately supportive, but occasionally volatile. When he flies off the handle, she retreats.

Why does Rockland stay? Because she loves her job. She travels frequently, and she has considerable autonomy and a great staff. Her decisions about huge budgets and investments count, and her contact with vendors brings her satisfaction.

But the issue of comparable worth eats at her: She wants to be equally valued—especially because she feels she works harder than the seven other directors (all men). Her annual review is coming up in five weeks. Can she get what she deserves, or is she going to have to find it elsewhere?

STRATEGY

AT the core of Rockland's dilemma is how cheaply valued she feels. Small wonder. She *is* undervalued. But the fault lies as much with her as with the company for allowing such a discrepancy to continue without protest. The situation is all too familiar. Even individuals who are savvy negotiators in business often are hesitant to negotiate for themselves. Rockland undervalues herself, and lets Perrone get away with doing the same, by continuing to try to "prove herself" and delaying her demands. Her hidden fear is that he'll retract his offer or fire her. So Rockland first must face herself—and shed her unrealistic hope that Perrone himself will recognize her worth and take care of her properly.

Good things occasionally do come to those who wait. But more often than not they go only to those who ask. Doing the job is the easier part of working. As you progress, the bigger—and more difficult—task is positioning and presenting yourself well. Making Perrone believe that Rockland is worth admitting to top management is akin to getting him to admit her to his private club. He and his colleagues agree that *they* belong, and they use their salaries and perks to prove it. Perrone has to acknowledge that Rockland belongs, too.

Rockland blows it when she runs scared and lets her boss manipulate her. She must learn how to negotiate for herself, an art that's a far cry from the kind of high-level capitulation she's been practicing. Negotiation requires that each side recognize what the other offers and be willing to trade for it. Like most bosses, Perrone wants the best and the most work done for the lowest price. He wants a fundamental conformity among his top staffers without having to manage and nurture them.

Rockland has power she doesn't recognize. She can deliver two jobs excellently. Without any real threat to herself, she can demonstrate that she's passed the competency test and warrants the title of vice president, and that she now is one of the elite and is entitled to top-level salary and perks.

Rockland also must remember to leave herself room to negotiate down. She has to ask for more than she really wants. That way she can generously give up some of her demands, allowing Perrone to save face.

Will Rockland get fired for asking? It's not likely. Is she being greedy by asking for more money when she already lives comfortably? Her cost of living is irrelevant to this case. What matters is how she stacks up against her peers in terms of prestige and importance in the company.

If Rockland doesn't stand up to Perrone and demand her due now, the consequences for her career may be dire: She'll keep playing director, but her authority and reputation will be tarnished. In time, colleagues may even wonder whether she's aggressive enough to handle her job, since she obviously is so lax about her own advancement. Rockland has no choice. She's got to take the chance—or take the bigger risk of getting bumped off the fast track. Like so many people, she hasn't understood that a dance is required in corporate life. Now's the time for her to learn the steps.

RECLASSIFICATION AS A STRATEGY FOR PROMOTION

Rockland should schedule a meeting with Perrone immediately, not wait until her review. What she should push for is, in effect, a reclassification.

ROCKLAND: Thanks a lot for taking the time to talk with me about our work together. We need to fix a broken situation. It seems there are some inequities in how the directors are compensated.

PERRONE: Oh no, I don't want to go into that now. Wait until your review.

ROCKLAND: Look at it as an opportunity to put things right early. You'll be as astonished as I was to see the major gaps in salary and perks among the directors: Seven of the eight have VP titles. The only one who doesn't heads two departments. Look at salaries: That same director gets paid the least. That's twice the work for two-thirds the pay. And stock options . . .

PERRONE: You know that Anderson, Billard, and Cohen all have larger departments.

ROCKLAND: Granted. The point is, they each have only one department to run. I have two and cover a larger client base than either of them. So let's say it's simply more work for less pay.

PERRONE: Well, they all have more experience under their belt.

ROCKLAND: So help me get the experience. The other directors all go to the quarterly council meetings where policy decisions are made. That means that two departments don't have adequate representation. My presence would help both of us make more informed decisions.

PERRONE: Look, Nina, you know the whole industry is having a rough time this year.

ROCKLAND: You're saving McHugh's salary already, since I've taken over his department. Ken, I think you're a great leader of a great company. And I want to stay. But my bank clients are wondering why "VP" isn't on my card when it is on theirs. It makes them feel that the company doesn't take their business seriously. It's time for you to show that you value my role here.

If Perrone refuses to compromise, Rockland has to have the courage to walk out, letting him worry about the next step. If he still doesn't give in to some of her demands, Rockland has to come to terms with her situation and consider another company. But it's more likely that he'll give in on the title (it won't cost anything) and on some of the other items.

You're Doing the Work: Can You Get the Title?

> Don't get mad—get ahead.
> This seemingly unfair situation can
> be your big break.

Almost from the day Liz Hamilton started her job, she found that her responsibilities extended way beyond her title. Hired as the assistant vice president in charge of travel sales for a large hotel corporation, Hamilton was in charge of selling and servicing national accounts. But she immediately began doing much of her boss's work, such as traveling on sales calls and conducting seminars. Karen Wehrhouse was happy to let Hamilton do some of her work, and Hamilton was grateful for the opportunity to take on new challenges. But lately Hamilton has begun to feel as if she is being taken advantage of. Last month, after nearly a year on the job, she asked Wehrhouse for a title change to vice president. Wehrhouse brushed her off, saying she wasn't ready.

But Wehrhouse has repeatedly praised Hamilton's work, and as for her being ready, she has been doing the job of vice president for eleven months! Through her extensive travel abroad, Hamilton has single-handedly increased sales by 120 percent. She has made it her business to personally welcome many of these new customers at the hotel and to handle any problems they might encounter. Her remarkable service often results in repeat business, a fact that certainly warrants more than a pat on the back.

All Hamilton wants is a title that reflects her responsibilities. And she does not understand why Wehrhouse and the company are withholding it when they know full well she has earned it.

She likes the work, but she can't be content without a title change. How can she get it? Should she stop doing the extra duties until she gets the title change? If she doesn't get the new title, should she ask for a transfer? Or should she leave the company altogether? Perhaps she is being petty and should forget the whole matter, as a friend has advised her. "What's important is what you do—not the sign over your door," he said.

☐ NEGOTIATING A NEW RANK ☐

Having assumed duties that are normally in the domain of a vice president, Hamilton has earned the title. When she asked Wehrhouse for a title change, her boss was evasive, telling her she wasn't ready. At first she felt hurt and angry; but now she is determined to find out what Wehrhouse's concerns are so she can address them directly.

HAMILTON: A little while ago I asked you to change my title from assistant vice president to vice president. You said at the time that you didn't think I was ready yet.

WEHRHOUSE: Yes. I also told you that you are doing a great job here and that in due course, if you continue to perform this well, a promotion would be in order.

HAMILTON: Well, I've been reflecting on what you said, and I've drawn up a list of what I was hired to do as an assistant VP and what I have been doing. Here it is. As you can see, I'm now doing the work of a vice president, and I love it. It really uses my best talents. I'm outperforming my competitors, and sales are up 120 percent.

So I've been wondering what concerns you might have about reclassifying me. Is it a budget problem?

WEHRHOUSE: Well, as you know, the industry is in a terrible slump right now, and we all hope it will improve soon. But until it does, I'm afraid our budget is frozen, and I won't be able to find the funds. In the meantime, I think you can see this is an opportunity to groom yourself for vice president.

HAMILTON: I've already done that. I'm doing the same job as those who have the title of vice president. It would help give me and the company more credibility if I had the title, too. To our European clients, titles are even more important than they are to us. They need me to be a VP in order to feel valued by our company.

I know this is a tight time. So I'm asking for a reward for my work that won't cost you anything. I'm willing to forgo a raise for now. What's more important to me is a title that accurately describes my responsibilities. All it does is confirm your faith in me, and it doesn't cost you a dime.

WEHRHOUSE: That's an interesting proposition. Let me think about it.

HAMILTON: My appraisal is due next month. Can we talk before then?

WEHRHOUSE: Absolutely.

STRATEGY

SOCIETY has always used titles to designate rank. In business, titles have been a denotation of status within the company and, in turn, have represented that measure to the outside world. Not surprisingly, then, impressive titles tend to be highly prized and sparingly bestowed.

An important-sounding title adds to our sense of self-worth. It is, after all, an acknowledgment of what we do, even when our duties are difficult to describe or ascribe worth to—a common problem in large organizations, where responsibilities are not readily apparent to others. In fact, in a study by Accountemps, a temporary-personnel agency, 60 percent of executives cited titles, second only to salaries, as the best indication of an employee's status.

So Hamilton should disregard her friend's advice: Titles are important and are worth striving for. And she does, indeed, deserve to be named vice president.

But to succeed in this effort, Hamilton needs a more sophisticated understanding of the politics of titles. Her sense that she is being taken advantage of is most likely unjustified—a symptom of her naïveté. Most managers get titles *after* they have been performing the duties of that title and have proved they can handle the new position. So for Hamilton to stop performing the extra duties until she receives a title change, or to perform them grudgingly, would be a losing career strategy.

Hamilton should approach her boss again, but this time as a mature professional, prepared to describe her point of view and negotiate from there. It's all too easy to misconstrue a boss's motives, to assume he or she gets a Scrooge-like glee from denying us our due. In most cases the boss's reasons for withholding a title change are far more complicated—and less malign.

Wehrhouse, for instance, may be worrying about a domino effect on other employees: If she promotes Hamilton to vice president, will her current vice president demand to be named a senior vice president? Or perhaps Wehrhouse is reluctant to give her a new title because she cannot offer her a raise. Or maybe she needs Hamilton to continue doing her assistant VP's duties and fears that the cost-conscious company wouldn't allow her to hire a new assistant if Hamilton were promoted. Hamilton needs to find out—either through the grapevine or by asking Wehrhouse directly—what factors may be influencing her. The more she understands her boss's constraints and concerns, the better she can address them and bring Wehrhouse around to her point of view.

When Hamilton does approach Wehrhouse again, she should point out that her counterparts in competing companies hold titles similar to the one she is asking for. She should also compare her original job description to what she is doing now, emphasizing both her gratitude for the opportunities she's had and her desire to accomplish more for the company.

She also might want to keep in mind a trend uncovered in the Accountemps study: While companies are giving smaller salary increases to employees, they are trying to compensate by shelling out more impressive titles. So her chances may be much better than she thinks.

If Wehrhouse still says no, Hamilton might ask for a tentative date for another review. In the interim, she should comfort herself with the knowledge that her challenging responsibilities are providing her with valuable experience—training for which graduate schools charge steep tuitions—that will undoubtedly help her take the next step in her career.

THE BAD BOSS: CAN YOU MAKE HIM BETTER?

> *If you're convinced you're in the right, think again. You could be looking at the situation all wrong.*

Nell Long is fed up. Long, a thirty-year-old management consultant in a multinational accounting firm, has always endured nit-picking criticism from her boss, Michael Sellers, but the situation has become unbearable.

In an hour-long meeting, Sellers berated Long for being a "perfectionist," claiming she was largely responsible for their division's 20 percent decline in profits. Sellers contended that Long had been spending too much on data research and collection. Long tried to explain that she could not arrive at intelligent recommendations without exhaustive research into her clients' situations. Frustrated, she reminded him that she had cleared this very course of action with him weeks ago. But, typically, Sellers wouldn't listen. Instead he told her that she wasn't doing her clients any favors, and that her perfectionism would stand in the way of her career advancement.

Long is certain that Sellers is wrong, as usual. All of her

co-workers think that Sellers is petty, sloppy, and incompetent, and a terrible listener. But what can she do? Sellers is her boss.

One co-worker advised her to put up with Sellers's criticism and not even consider appealing to his superior, Diane Everett. "You'll never change Sellers," her colleague said.

But to Long that course of action seems too passive—not to mention unfair. After all, Long would like to be recognized and rewarded for her good work. She wonders what would happen if she were to confront Sellers and explain to him exactly how she feels she has been mistreated. Would he apologize? Or would he retaliate? Perhaps she should just quit and find another job with a better boss.

☐ GETTING YOUR SUPERIORS ☐ ON YOUR SIDE

When Nell Long's boss, Michael Sellers, criticizes her for being a perfectionist and spending too much time on data collecting, she can respond in a number of ways. But only one will serve to advance her career. Here are four possible responses; try to figure out which is the best.

1. "Our very business is based on how well we can service our clients, isn't it? How can doing that job for our clients hurt us? I think I am doing what I'm supposed to be doing. But if you prefer another mode of working, well, you're the boss . . ."
2. "Of course, you're right. I am really sorry. I will behave differently on the next project. If you want, I will check in at the midway point, just to make sure I'm doing everything right. I do want your guidance and trust."
3. "I resent your criticism. Data collection is the core of our business. Not only am I not overdoing it, but I think our department doesn't do enough. I can prove my point

by having you talk to some of my clients. Far from being too much of a perfectionist, you will find that I am doing the job the way it should be done."

4. "Point taken, Michael. You probably are right in that I am a compulsive researcher, but I need to be certain of my facts before I can make a recommendation. I will, however, try to conduct speedier investigations in the future. I must say, I'm glad that this is your only beef, because it isn't a fatal flaw. I can bring my billable hours down."

The first response is self-righteous and self-destructive; clinging to the fact that she is right will serve only to exacerbate tensions between her and Sellers. Likewise, the second reaction—groveling—is unproductive; it will only make Long resentful and set her up as a weak player in the company. The third answer would be suicidal. It would antagonize Sellers and place them in enemy camps. The fourth is the best response. By standing up for her work yet appreciating her boss's point of view, Long will be able to develop a working relationship with him.

☐   ☐

STRATEGY

To most of us the word *boss* has negative connotations, suggesting oppression and tyranny. If you look up the word in the *Oxford English Dictionary*, however, you may be surprised to learn that it is neutral in origin. It comes from the Dutch and means "master" or "uncle." The word also has German roots, signifying "aunt." But say "boss" aloud a few times and the word takes on a negative hue. Let's face it: To most of us a boss is somebody we must please. And that can become a full-time job in itself.

In Long's case it certainly has. I agree with Long—she has a bad boss. And like most bad bosses, he doesn't listen. But Long probably won't like my advice any better than that of her colleague. I know from experience that she is pursuing a destructive course by insisting that she is right and Sellers is wrong. Giving in to her impulse to defend herself against his accusations may feel liberating at the moment, but I can promise it will cost her heavily later. There is no way for her to win this fight; the other side is too well armed.

Long's complaints notwithstanding, Sellers is not a reflective sort; most likely he isn't capable of seeing how he appears to Long and the rest of his staff. And the truth is, he doesn't have to be concerned with that. All his superiors want him to do is behave in the way they deem appropriate and make sure that his division meets its deadlines and lives within its budget. And that is exactly what Sellers is doing.

Appealing to Everett, then, would not only be fruitless but could potentially be devastating. Everett probably handpicked Sellers precisely because he acts in a way that she and other top managers in the firm consider desirable. Long's complaint would only isolate her as a whiner and a weak employee who is unable to take the heat. She might even set herself up to be laid off or fired.

What Long can and should do is ask herself why Sellers is hypercritical. The bad boss rarely thinks he or she is bad. You can be sure Sellers has reasons for acting the way he does, although he may not be able to articulate them. Perhaps he is feeling pressure from Everett and is lashing out as a way of protecting himself. Or maybe he is having family difficulties, so his fuse is short. Of course, none of this would excuse his conduct, but by understanding Sellers's underlying concerns, Long will be able to respond in a way that might alleviate them.

There's another significant aspect to Long's dilemma: her own anger. Why is she so enraged by Sellers's criticism? Is it because she senses some truth in it? That's a question everyone should consider when a boss levels criticism. In Long's case, she may be religiously researching subjects because she is still waging that age-old female battle for acceptance; she's terrified of being wrong. But there's nothing wrong with being wrong occasionally. Long should allow herself to make mistakes and then move on, just like those at the top. Lower-level employees tend to be more defensive and more insistent upon being "right"; at higher levels, where managers take bigger chances for greater stakes, they argue less with their bosses and concentrate instead on forging postitive relationships based on trust.

Finally, Long should consider how much she enjoys her work. She likes her job and sees many advantages in being associated with one of the world's largest accounting firms. In fact, the only troublesome aspect of her job is Sellers.

Therefore, a possible solution is to find another boss inside the firm. Quitting would be throwing the baby out with the bath water—an expression coined, no doubt, from the multitude of instances in which angry, frustrated people just chucked the whole situation rather than change one irksome aspect of it.

One step in finding a new boss is finding a mentor within the company. Long should try to find a high-ranking, influential manager in the firm whom she respects. She has every opportunity for advancement if she can become a corporate pole-vaulter. Replacing Sellers, rather than fighting him, is her best strategy.

In the meantime, Long needs to get along with Sellers. That doesn't mean silently suffering his barbs. She should acknowledge his concerns and assure him that she will work on them, but she should not become a lapdog—subservience won't get her into upper management.

Developing a healthy relationship with a boss is among the most important career-building skills women can learn. But it is also the most trying, for the boss's power, coupled with our own dependence, spawns an extraordinarily intricate relationship.

CAN YOU
BREAK INTO THE INNER
CIRCLE?

> You don't need to be your
> boss's buddy, but you do need
> to be on the same wavelength.
> How to tune in.

Mary Jo Bensinger, an assistant corporate-affairs manager for a multinational manufacturer, increasingly feels as though she has been shut out of the inner circle. There has been no single dramatic event, no blowup or brouhaha—rather, just an unsettling sense that she isn't one of those favored by the boss.

Ever since Bensinger joined the department fourteen months ago, she has watched her boss, Jeanette Toomey, lavish attention and encouragement on her two "stars" while Bensinger has gotten only perfunctory acknowledgement. Toomey takes her pets out for long, leisurely lunches to discuss new projects. Bensinger gets a ten-minute meeting, with instructions delivered rapid-fire. She wondered if she was being overly sensitive—until last week at a staff meeting, when Toomey abruptly interrupted her explanation of a new policy with a dismissive remark and then conspicuously changed the subject.

Bensinger knows she is talented and capable. At previous

jobs, she was on the fast track. That's why her current situation is so difficult to bear. She sorely misses the attention and perks that came with being in the inner circle.

At first it seemed as though her problems stemmed from being a new employee. But even after fourteen months, the situation has not improved. She is losing confidence and becoming inhibited.

A friend advised her to seek a transfer, saying the "chemistry isn't right" and "you can't fix chemistry." Bensinger dismissed the suggestion because she is at a growing company, working in a department with an excellent reputation. She wanted to make the job work. But now she wonders: Is that possible?

☐ # THE WORDS TO SAY: GETTING PERSONAL— PROFESSIONALLY ☐

After an unusually contentious staff meeting in which staff members could not agree on a proposal, Bensinger finds herself alone with her boss, senior vice president Jeanette Toomey. In the past, she would have fled, feeling insecure around Toomey. But today Bensinger recognizes—and seizes—the opportunity to show off a strength she knows Toomey will value.

BENSINGER: I was surprised by the lack of consensus. Were you?

TOOMEY: Yes—and concerned. We've got a deadline. We've got to resolve this soon or we'll be in big trouble.

BENSINGER: You know, building consensus happens to be a great interest of mine. I spent some time in business school studying methods to achieve it.

TOOMEY: Really? Anything you'd like to pass on?

BENSINGER: Well, the main thing is—as you already stress in meetings—to develop clear alternatives that people can evaluate. If you want, I could draw up three alternatives based on the comments that people made today and present them at the next meeting.

TOOMEY: That would be very helpful. Why don't you draft some ideas and then come by my office Thursday so we can discuss them before you write anything up.

BENSINGER: Great!

TOOMEY: Thanks for bringing this up. It'll be a great help, Mary Jo.

BENSINGER: No problem. By the way, I saw an article in the Sunday paper about how to make your house more attractive to prospective buyers. It had some interesting ideas. Did you see it—or would you like me to give you a copy?

TOOMEY: No, I didn't see it. Would you mind sending it my way? We could use all the help we can get. I'm beginning to think we ought to take the house off the market for a while, until things turn around.

BENSINGER: That seems to be a common complaint these days. But this article has some interesting tips. I'll bring it up on Thursday.

☐   ☐

STRATEGY

MANY of us have found ourselves on the outside of the inner circle. It's a painful position to be in. In this situation, people tend to fall into one of three response styles: They become sycophants, begging for admission to the club; they assume a haughty air, rejecting those who rejected them; or they simply withdraw, as Bensinger has done. These responses are, however, merely defensive postures. None of them will solve the problem. They may, in fact, fuel it.

Running away to a new job isn't the answer either. No matter where Bensinger goes, she will be faced with the necessity of being part of the inner circle if she wants to be successful. Instead of flying the coop, then, she needs to put aside her injured feelings and bruised ego and pursue Toomey and her clique. The fact is, she has to learn to make them appreciate her. How? By demonstrating that she is one of them, not an outsider.

Feelings of being different or second-best start with childhood. Sibling rivalry doesn't end when we become adults. Look at any group and watch how the team members vie for the attention and favor of the leader. If a childhood pattern of not belonging overwhelms our behavior in our professional life, then psychotherapy becomes a necessary tool to uncover and untangle the unresolved childhood issues.

But often the feelings are based on reality: We really *are* different. We may be more or less intellectual, emotional, or motivated than our colleagues or supervisor. In those situations, we have to develop a complementary style and make our differences assets, in order to belong and be valued.

Bensinger is more analytical and intellectual than Toomey. She likes to ruminate. Toomey tends to be decisive and quick on the draw. In meetings she makes snap decisions: "Let's do it!" Bensinger prefers to study an issue and mull over the possibilities. Bensinger needs to figure out where she is *too* different from Toomey, and be willing to adapt or her career will suffer. She has resisted doing this because, inwardly, she regards Toomey's seat-of-the-pants approach as superficial. And to Toomey, Bensinger's serious style is ponderous and pompous.

Chitchatting and schmoozing obviously are important tactics (see, in Part Three, "The Power of Small Talk: How to

Schmooze Successfully"). Because she feels threatened, Bensinger has steered clear of small talk, becoming even more cerebral than usual. She should try to become conscious of this habit.

Toomey's style does have its virtues. The department has a good reputation partly because of Toomey's ability to get things done quickly and efficiently. Bensinger needs to recognize the positive aspects of Toomey's style. Part of succeeding is recognizing how your superiors work and finding a way to compliment it. That doesn't mean "selling out" or giving up treasured and valued aspects of yourself. Instead, it requires figuring out what your superiors and colleagues value and acting in a way that will enable them to appreciate your talent. Sometimes that will mean mirroring their behavior.

For example, instead of coming to meetings to hash out issues, as Bensinger prefers, the two stars come with carefully prepared reports that Toomey can respond to on the spot. Bensinger should do the same. If she wants to ruminate, she can do it before the meeting.

Ideally, Toomey will become for Bensinger what every rising executive needs: a mentor, someone who can help her understand the machinery of the organization so she can climb through the ranks. In my experience, I have found that everyone who has succeeded in the corporate world has done so with the help of a mentor. A mentor provides the safe way of learning the inner workings of that world. As Bensinger climbs the corporate ladder, this kind of information will become critical.

But if Bensinger and Toomey never develop the level of rapport that evolves into mentorship, Bensinger should then conduct a mentor search. A mentor should be a high-level, influential officer whose talents and style mesh with yours. You can't just ask the person to be your mentor; you have to invest time and energy in developing a relationship. That might mean working overtime on the mentor's pet project or volunteering to assume a new duty. But the hard work will pay off. You will adapt to the corporate style and learn how to speak the language top managers speak.

This education will become useful later in your career, when *you* take on the role of mentor and teach the rules of the game to your protégé. By that time you'll have learned that adapting to your boss's style doesn't mean selling out; it means finding a way to weave yourself into the corporate fabric so you can show your talents off to their best advantage.

WHY IT DOESN'T MATTER THAT YOUR BOSS DOESN'T LIKE YOU

> Y*ou'll never be buddies, but you can become allies. Here's how.*

Emily Crane left work frustrated again. An accountant for a steel company, she had slaved over a memo to her boss, Elliot Graves, analyzing in detail the ways in which the firm could take advantage of a new tax law. Not only did Graves not thank her for her work, he barely acknowledged receiving it. "Haven't read it yet," he grunted when she politely asked what he had thought of it.

It wasn't the first time he had brushed her off. In the year that Crane has worked for Graves, she's often delivered lengthy memos, and Graves has rarely bothered to respond. Frequently he has given her the last dibs on assignments. At first Crane thought that she was to blame; somehow her work must be lacking. She read all the trade journals to keep on top of trends and sent him copies of the articles that she thought he would find interesting. She checked and double-checked reports before handing them in and made sure that they were exhaustive. But nothing changed.

Then she tried convincing herself that his unpleasantness was *his* problem. After all, her previous bosses had liked her—a lot. Her last manager, who supervised her work for four years, had become such a good friend that Crane was a bridesmaid at her wedding. Graves is just brusque and inconsiderate, she told herself; he doesn't know how to get along with people.

But lately Crane has found it harder and harder to ignore the slights, especially when she looks around and sees that she is the only one in the four-person department whom Graves treats poorly. The fact is, Graves doesn't like her. There is no "chemistry" between them. The question is, what can she do about it? Crane is, by nature, a studious and serious person; her boss is boisterous, impatient, and impulsive. How can she create this chemistry where there is none?

Crane would quit if she could, but it's a particularly bad time to look. Her husband is afraid he'll be laid off, the economy is still lousy, and there are few corporations in her area that can match her present salary and benefits package. Meanwhile Graves's chilly indifference is beginning to affect Crane's self-esteem and enthusiasm, and she's afraid to make mistakes. She wonders: Is there any way to change his mind about her?

WINNING HIM OVER: SEVEN WAYS

At some point you will work for a boss who doesn't like you. You probably won't be able to turn him into your best friend, but you don't need to. All that is necessary is that he feel comfortable around you and respect your work. Here are seven ways to make that happen.

- Identify the tasks or projects that matter most to your boss and be extraordinarily productive in those areas.
- Help him overcome work-related crises.

- Observe the work habits and styles of his favored subordinates. Do they have a casual approach? Or are they likely to communicate by memo? Follow their lead.
- Analyze why you have been behaving differently. Are you unconsciously replicating an unhealthy relationship you may have had in the past? Does your supervisor remind you of another authority figure with whom you didn't get along?
- Ask colleagues whom you trust to share their insights with you. Listen with an open mind.
- If your boss continues to rebuff you, arrange a friendly meeting with him. Tell him that you sense tension and want to resolve it. Ask him in what ways you are not meeting his expectations.
- Keep in mind that you can't change your boss. But you can change your interactions with him.

☐   ☐

STRATEGY

CRANE is focusing on the wrong question. The issue isn't whether she can make her boss like her but whether she can make him respect her. Women, having been trained to be charming and nice, often pour their energies into making people like them; even though they crave being valued for their abilities, they have learned to hide behind a mask of amiability and subservience. And sometimes this strategy pays off.

But the higher you rise in the corporate hierarchy, the less likely it is to be effective. In the upper echelons, being well liked isn't nearly as crucial as being respected and appreciated. Middle- and upper-level managers aren't expected to be helpmates but rather team players, people who contribute to corporate goals in such a way that they prove they "fit in." If they become their bosses' pals in the process, that's a plus, but it's not a requirement.

Of course, proving that you fit in isn't always easy. There is an element of what Crane calls "chemistry," though it is not as mysterious as she suggests. In the best circumstances, it develops without any effort; the employee and manager instinctively understand each other. It sounds as if Crane is lucky enough to have enjoyed that situation before. But chemistry is relatively rare. In fact, many management problems I've studied stem not from poor work performance but from interpersonal difficulties. In my experience, the most successful professionals in corporate organizations usually have an ability to develop a rapport where there was none; they have been able to forge bonds with people with whom they had little in common. They never became buddies, but they did become allies. Crane can do the same.

First, though, she needs to figure out why Graves is so ill at ease around her. To begin, Crane must determine what Graves expects from his employees in terms of work and behavioral style. She can do that by reading the clues, observing whom and what he responds to. What are the colleagues he likes doing that she isn't? What does she do that they don't?

My guess is that Crane's problem lies in her style, not her work. She has always been an achiever; there is no reason to suspect that her performance is slipping now. Crane is methodical and attentive to detail, producing lengthy, involved reports. Graves, on the other hand, is impulsive and impatient, preferring to act spontaneously. Her style may be irritating to him. Do other staffers give Graves brief, to-the-point memos that he can digest in a few minutes? Do they just drop in, verbally conveying what they have discovered? Crane needs to pick up on these clues.

At the same time, she must ask herself why she has allowed the relationship to deteriorate. Instead of figuring out what Graves wanted and how she could supply it, Crane blamed herself, burying herself in her work. This is a common reaction (especially among women, who are accustomed to assuming culpability), but inevitably it is counterproductive, serving only to anger both the boss and the employee. When Crane attempted to deny the importance of the relationship, shifting from "I'm nothing" to "He's nothing," it was equally futile. No one, especially a manager, can tolerate being ignored.

Crane needs to decide whether she is unconsciously sabotaging herself. Does Graves remind her of an authority figure from her past with whom she had difficulty? Before she can change her behavior, she must understand her underlying motivations.

What if she makes changes and still the relationship doesn't improve? Then she should turn to one or two trusted co-workers. They will probably have insights into the situation and be willing to share them. She must be prepared to hear them without being defensive. Later she can weigh the responses and determine which have merit.

There is always the chance that what Graves sees as a flaw is something Crane cannot change. I know of managers who have resented staffers because they resemble their ex-wives or mothers. Similarly, I know of a boss who is partial to women staffers who are dark-haired and wear Brooks Brothers dresses—just like his wife. Short of altering her appearance (a strategy I wouldn't advise but that isn't unheard of), Crane is left with little choice but to talk to her boss.

The setting should be casual; if possible, the meeting should seem spontaneous. Crane should speak carefully so as not to seem accusing. She should ask straightforward questions that don't ascribe blame. Instead of saying, "You're always ignoring me," she might say, "I feel some tension between us. Are my memos too long? What can I do to make the situation better?" Her aim should be to force her boss to lay out the ground rules, establishing what is expected of her professionally. That will make him focus on her performance and will give both of them specific guidelines to follow. Crane should make sure to end the discussion on a positive note; no one likes big, dramatic confrontations.

If the relationship fails to improve, Crane may have to find a new job. But that is an unlikely scenario. Once she demonstrates that she understands her manager, a bond will develop based on mutual appreciation for work well done. They may never like each other, but they will learn to respect each other.

SHOULD
YOU BE YOUR
BOSS'S BUDDY?

O*ffice romances aren't
the only work relationships that
can be troubling.*

Caroline Shaffer is still amazed by her predicament. After years of working for insensitive, self-involved supervisors, she is now faced with the dilemma of having a boss who is *too* friendly. Ever since Shaffer was promoted six months ago to vice president of the human-resources department of a major utilities company, her manager, Marlene Hardy, has been actively cultivating Shaffer's friendship.

Hardy, the department's senior vice president, had always been cordial to Shaffer, sharing business articles and books with her, offering tickets to plays and concerts when she couldn't use them. But lately she's been treating Shaffer more like a friend than a colleague. Unlike most of the firm's upper management, Shaffer and Hardy are both single. Hardy, having recently ended her eight-year marriage, is developing an active social life, and she is trying to make Shaffer a part of it. Just this week she invited Shaffer to her beach house for Saturday brunch to help her plan a large dinner party. Last week she asked Shaffer to go to a party with her.

Shaffer accepted both invitations and enjoyed herself, as she always does with Hardy. Her boss is smart and interesting and has many well-connected friends, to whom she introduces Shaffer. Still, Shaffer is worried about their growing closeness. Brought up to respect the line between business and pleasure, she is accustomed to keeping a polite distance from supervisors, careful never to overstep the bounds of propriety. She feels uncomfortable doing otherwise.

What if Hardy has ulterior motives? While Shaffer respects her boss, she does not completely trust her. Hardy is one of the most aggressive and ambitious people she has ever known. In fact, she has been engaged in a turf war with another department head for months. She could be hoping to use Shaffer, whose reputation as a straight arrow is well known, as her ally. Also, Hardy is rumored to be losing favor with top management; she might be trying to build support. Would it be unwise for Shaffer to align herself with her now? And what if she and Hardy became better acquainted and then discovered that they did not like each other? Would Shaffer's job be in jeopardy?

THE DOS AND DON'TS: A QUIZ

If you are fortunate enough to have a boss who wants to befriend you, take up the offer—carefully. Below, test your ability to handle it.

1. *Your boss confides in you about a political battle she is having with her superior. At a charity function, you find yourself seated next to her arch enemy. Teasingly, he pumps you for information about her. You:*

A. Ignore his prodding and talk about everything else—
the charity or current events.

B. Remind him of your commitment to your boss and
her achievements.

C. Try to reconcile their differences, telling him they
could be powerful allies.

ANSWER: A. B will mark you as a humorless sycophant
and possibly close off a future ally. C is noble but futile,
and a bit naive; no one changes another's opinion in
that kind of setting. A is the safest response, particularly
if you can joke back.

2. *Your boss is single. She asks you to introduce her to an*
eligible male. You:

A. Agree and invite her to your next party.

B. Politely refuse, explaining that it lies outside the
bounds of your job.

C. Make excuses to hide your reluctance.

ANSWER: A. B is narrow-minded. What is the harm in
letting her meet an acquaintance? If she is too needy,
try C.

3. *At a large staff meeting, your boss is attacked by a rival.*
Your boss ardently defends herself and then looks to you
for back-up. You:

A. Take up the challenge and argue your boss's case
further.

B. Pretend to misread her signal so that you aren't
caught in the cross fire.

C. Stake out a middle ground with a compromising
position.

ANSWER: A. You are in a true dilemma; none of your
options is good. With A, you are being loyal, but if your
boss loses, you may lose, too. B means letting your boss
down; she may not forget it—and she may not lose. C
sounds smart, but if you play mediator without anyone's

invitation, you'll look like a wimp who caved in. So choose A, and be as diplomatic as possible.

☐   ☐

STRATEGY

MANY of us learned the maxim "Don't mix business with pleasure," but that is dead wrong: Often, business is pleasure. Mixing the two by befriending colleagues not only makes work more pleasant but also fosters success, especially as people accrue responsibility and rely increasingly on their ability to work well with others.

In general, men are more familiar with this lesson, having been tutored in the unspoken rules of the corporate world from an early age. As a result, they often invest considerable time, energy, and money in building business connections. They create work-related rituals—weekly poker games or Saturday golf outings—in the hopes of developing strong relationships with co-workers and bosses.

Shaffer is fortunate. She doesn't have to expend that kind of effort. She already works for someone who is bright, well connected, and exceedingly eager to share her contacts. Most men would jump at such an offer. So should she.

But she is right to be wary: Friendships with managers are fraught with peril. I've seen many cases in which supervisors have cultivated relationships with their talented underlings for less-than-altruistic reasons. Some hurt those close to them through self-destructive behavior; others used their people for Machiavellian plots. Hardy may indeed want to use Shaffer to help win a political battle. It is also possible, however, that Hardy is befriending her for more benign reasons. After all, they do share common interests; they are both single, smart, and ambitious, and Shaffer admits that they have fun together. Hardy could turn out to be the ideal business buddy, a confidante, mentor, and trusted ally—or she could be the friend from hell. Shaffer won't know until she tests the relationship. Either way, she needs to protect herself in case her fears are justified. How?

First, Shaffer should try to search out Hardy's history. Does she have a pattern of using her underlings for nefarious purposes? Is she known for being overly needy or mean-spirited? Even if Shaffer doesn't run across any smoking guns, she still needs to proceed cautiously. A friendship with a boss is never a friendship in the classic sense of a bond between equals, a mutual and honest sharing of feelings, wishes, and fears. Shaffer is the subordinate: Hardy will always retain power over her.

Therefore, Shaffer should not reciprocate by inviting Hardy to join her social group. Nor should she always speak frankly. Instead, she must be a sympathetic sounding board, tempering her candor with the recognition that she *is* talking to her supervisor, no matter how friendly the circumstances. She cannot forget that whatever she tells Hardy can be used against her. Even if Hardy is the most virtuous person in the world, she may feel forced to break confidences if the company or her professional well-being is involved. Shaffer shouldn't reveal sensitive information that might put Hardy in the position of having to choose between Shaffer and her job. She should also be politic about disclosing her opinion on company matters, to ensure that Hardy doesn't have any ammunition to use against her should their friendship dissolve.

And what should she do if her worst suspicions are confirmed? She will need to extricate herself—gradually. She might begin by, say, declining every other dinner invitation, always offering a polite and plausible excuse and suggesting lunch during the work week instead. If Hardy tries to involve her in a losing political scheme, Shaffer should position herself as a neutral observer, refrain from giving input or support, and limit her role to that of an interested listener. Will Hardy's feelings be hurt? Probably. But if Shaffer has been discreet and cautious in dissolving the relationship, Hardy will probably not be able to hurt her career.

There is another potential problem that Shaffer should watch for. She needs to guard against co-workers who may be envious and resentful of her relationship with their boss. Sibling-like rivalry isn't limited to families. To minimize friction, Shaffer should be careful not to appear to be flaunting her special access to Hardy. Unless asked, she should not discuss the parties or events she attends with the boss. And she should never, ever, use Hardy to punish her enemies. Not only would that be an abuse of Hardy's trust, but it almost certainly would backfire on her. Shaffer needs the respect and good will of her peers as well as her boss.

Having a close relationship with a supervisor can be an invaluable experience, enabling an employee to develop contacts, get a close-up view of how management decisions are made, try out her role as second-in-command, and possibly even gain a lifelong friend. The fact is that every boss has favorites, and when the chemistry is right, some turn out to be lasting allies—both inside and outside the office.

Confronting

Your Boss

> Standing up to a superior
> is like walking through a minefield,
> but you can do it without
> declaring war.

Judy Thompson, assistant vice president of finance at an aerospace company, is at her breaking point. Two months ago, her boss, Jim Packer, the vice president of finance, divested her of sole control over the budget, telling her that she would be sharing this responsibility with Louise Wood, a new assistant vice president. "I think this arrangement will work well. Wood ought to be real helpful to you," he said.

Not being the type to pick a fight, Thompson decided not to protest, although she didn't think she needed help, at least not the kind that Wood could provide. After just two weeks of working with Wood, Thompson has concluded that either she was recommended by a colleague to whom Packer owed a favor or she deserves an Oscar for her performance during the job interview. She is unable to do even basic financial analysis or numbers crunching. Thompson is doing all of the work; Wood spends her time chatting on the phone with friends. If that wasn't bad enough, yesterday Thompson saw Wood's paycheck stub lying on her desk and learned that Wood is earning more than she is—$10,250 more, to be exact.

"You have no choice," her friend John Rockwell told her. "You've got to confront Packer and demand a raise. And you've got to put Wood in her place. You can't be nice anymore." Thompson agrees she has to take action, but she feels intimidated and uncertain. Packer doesn't like to hear complaints—Thompson once overheard him calling one woman a "whiner" for coming to him with one too many gripes. As for Wood, she is extremely arrogant, refusing to take any advice from Thompson. "I know what I'm doing," Wood snapped once, when Thompson suggested an easier way to do a calculation.

Thompson wishes she were like the men in her office who brag about telling off their bosses and colleagues. But the truth is, she dreads conflict and doesn't share her feelings unless invited to do so. On the other hand, she knows she must speak out.

☐ DEFENDING YOURSELF: ☐ FOUR SCENARIOS

Do you shy away from conflict, or fight too hard? Check your reflexes and learn how to protect yourself without losing your professionalism.

1. *In your performance review, your boss rates your handling of new responsibilities a four out of a possible five. Insulted that your efforts are not appreciated, you question the score. "Nobody gets a five," she says. "Four is the highest I give."*

SOLUTION: Ask her to add a note on the bottom of the form indicating that four is the best score she gives, five being only a motivator. This will demonstrate that you want to advance in the company.

2. *A pet idea of yours has been approved but then is assigned to a co-worker.*

SOLUTION: Talk directly to your boss and find out precisely why he delegated responsibility for the project to someone else. Stress that you are willing to make whatever changes he thinks are necessary in your performance to regain control of your project—and then live up to your word.

3. *Your colleague has been badmouthing you to important clients. At first you figured people would consider the source, but now you've heard that some are actually taking his charges seriously.*

SOLUTION: Tell your colleague that you are upset by his actions and that you are going to talk to his boss if he persists in slandering you. To show him you mean business, take notes during your conversation.

4. *Your client hasn't been paying his bills despite promises to do so.*

SOLUTION: Call your client and propose a biweekly payment plan, and be dogged in enforcing it. If that doesn't work, consider settling for a smaller amount. Lawsuits rarely satisfy anyone involved.

STRATEGY

ROCKWELL is right—Thompson must confront her boss. But he is wrong in suggesting that it will necessitate a shouting match or a showdown. There are ways to stand up for yourself without being antagonizing and to meet the needs of both sides. Confrontation does not have to mean aggression, although many people assume that it does.

Men are conditioned to accept conflict as routine. For centuries, the ruling classes have been made up of men who directed their hostilities outwardly and learned to respect dominance and hierarchical relationships. Until recently, women were excluded from these socializing experiences. As a result, they often see confrontation as frightening, a daring act that can lead to their being despised, cast aside, or, subconsciously, even physically harmed. They cling to traditionally female patterns of behavior, rarely voicing disagreement, always trying to be cheerful, helpful, and accommodating. They are "nice"; consequently, their needs often aren't met—or even known.

While men usually aren't penalized for following stereotypical roles, "good girls" like Thompson can be. They are taken less seriously and seen as weak. Meanwhile, those women who assume male postures are often punished for their transgression. They are stigmatized for their brazenness, branded as pushy, manipulative, or "bitchy." (Similarly, men who exhibit feminine qualities are sometimes called wimps.)

Both the male and the female roles are deficient. The most successful strategy for men *and* women is to combine the best of both styles so that they are responsible and sympathetic to others' needs as well as their own. As corporate hierarchies are flattened, I believe more people will adopt this interactive approach. But until then, women face a particularly difficult problem: how to assert themselves without alienating anyone, particularly their male bosses.

Thompson should have confronted her boss the minute he announced that Wood would be co-managing the project. It is entirely possible that Wood's assignment is unrelated to Packer's feelings about Thompson. In that case, an expression of dismay might have been enough to convince Packer not to follow through with his plan. Even if the worst was true and Thompson was not able to change his mind, she would at least have been able to work out a plan to improve her performance, which eventually would lead to pay parity.

But what should Thompson do now? She must immediately set up a meeting with Packer to discuss her concerns (except salary, for reasons I will explain). She should rehearse beforehand so she will speak coherently and dispassionately. If women often avoid confrontations with men because they subconsciously fear violence, many men avoid face-offs with women because they fear an emotional outburst, especially tears. Not only do men not know how to respond to such a situation, they tend to resent it. The bottom line: Extreme emotions of any kind, including anger, are off-limits.

Once in the meeting, Thompson needs to ask polite but direct questions, such as, "I wonder why you felt that it was necessary to assign Wood to this project? Were you dissatisfied with my work in any way?" Her goal should be to come out with a clear idea of how she can better meet Packer's needs. Raising specific questions will force Packer to respond in kind and will demonstrate her commitment to accommodating him. Overreacting by issuing ultimatums or demands will only turn her boss into an adversary. (As for her male office mates' claims of bullying their bosses, I would doubt it; most men know enough to wage war laterally, not upward.)

But Thompson should take careful note of Packer's derision of a colleague as a "whiner." While Packer might have been guilty of stereotyping (would he ever accuse a man of whining?), there is an important lesson to be learned here: Managers don't want to hear complaints; they want solutions. Employees who come armed with them are seen as mature, reliable, and useful. Those who don't are nuisances and troublemakers.

Instead of saying, "I don't like working with Wood; she's incompetent," Thompson should explain how the relationship could be restructured. She could even suggest weekly goals for herself *and* Wood, explaining, "Since time is of the essence and we seem to be lagging behind schedule, I thought we might divide the duties this way. What do you think?"

If Packer accepts her plan, all she needs to do is to manage

Wood by enforcing strict deadlines. If Wood objects, Thompson can return to Packer. But if he rejects her original plan and suggests one of his own, she should adhere to it closely, confident that he will be watching Wood carefully. A cautionary note: If Packer's solution doesn't work, Thompson should resist the temptation to say "I told you so." And if Packer turns out to be right? Admit it.

As to the question of pay, Thompson should negotiate for a raise only after she has met Packer's expectations with concrete results. She should remind him of her accomplishments, alluding to Wood's salary only if he seems resistant or tries to underpay her: "I've heard that others at my level earn $10,000 more than I do." If he still refuses to give her what she is worth, then she should look for another job—quietly.

Thompson has a responsibility and a right to speak up for herself and protect her interests. But the best way for her to do that is not through hostile silence or angry threats; it's through clear, cool reasoning.

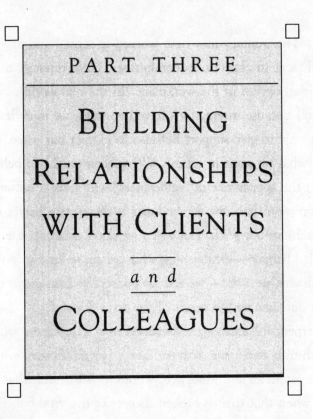

PART THREE

BUILDING RELATIONSHIPS WITH CLIENTS

and

COLLEAGUES

hen we were young we hoped that everyone would be caring and friendly. Eventually we learned that the world of relationships also included rejection, jealousy, and betrayal. Instead of learning to cope with such calamities, we often chose simply to leave the offending group and join another. As a result, we never learned how to trade for a better deal for ourselves. We never learned to negotiate with others for what we wanted.

This strategy may have worked in school and may still work in clubs or on committees. Unfortunately it isn't an option in the workplace. In the real world of work, because interactions have two sides, we must learn not only to give support but also to extract our price, to get what we want in return. We've been taught to believe that the appearance of "selflessness" will make a better impression than any demand and is therefore a better way to achieve our goals. But when we don't establish the so-called bargain—establishing what *we* are willing to give and what *we* want—we end up poorer, both in terms of the outcome and in terms of the meta-skills of interpersonal exchanges. Learning how to compete with both men and other women, how to establish our own competencies and influence, whom to trust, and what to do when that trust is broken, is part of the vital but invisible process of work.

In this section, we focus on how to make the most of the interactions that will define your *workplace*, your *workstyle*, your *worklife*.

The Power of Small Talk: How to Schmooze Successfully

> Small talk isn't just trivial chatter. It's a way to build trust and loyalty among colleagues.

Nikki Strom, an account executive with a midsize advertising agency, just got an invitation to a glitzy party celebrating the company's thirtieth anniversary, and her first reaction was, "How do I get out of this?" Though Strom is smart, talented, and dedicated to her work, she feels inept at the kind of small talk these situations demand. She's never been able to think of clever one-liners or funny anecdotes. Instead she finds herself either talking too much about work or, worse, not saying anything at all.

Take last week, for example, when Strom was on a flight to Cleveland with her boss, Ron DiBiasi. She buried herself in reading. She thought of trying to chitchat with him but wasn't sure how to get started or, for that matter, if it was even appropriate—DiBiasi seemed engrossed in the report on his lap. Besides, having a light conversation with DiBiasi would not be easy. The two had never had a great rapport.

Just one month earlier, he had promoted Strom's only true peer, an account executive who has virtually the same background and experience as hers. One key difference between them: Her peer is charming and able to make the normally mirthless DiBiasi laugh.

At Strom's informal agency, there is a lot of time for small talk. Strom sees herself as serious-minded and doesn't partake in it, even with subordinates. To her, schmoozing is superficial talk that dazzles and distracts people from real, substantive matters.

Strom realizes, however, that this party is a chance for her to recover from the dreary airplane flight and improve relations with her boss, if only she can figure out what to say.

☐ THE ART OF CHITCHAT ☐

Everyone, even the most accomplished executive, appreciates a chance to talk about himself or herself, and people especially like to talk about their hobbies. Since Strom—and everyone else in the agency—knows that her boss, Ron DiBiasi, is a dedicated poker player (who is on a winning streak), she should ask him about it. To converse successfully, all she needs is a thoughtful opening question, follow-up question, and a few sincere words of praise.

Scene:
The bar at the company's
thirtieth anniversary party.

STROM: What a great party. And what a great reason to celebrate—thirty years!

DIBIASI: Yes. Sometimes I wasn't sure we'd make it.

STROM: It took sacrifices. Speaking of which, aren't you missing your poker game to be here?

DIBIASI (*laughs*): No, that's Tuesday.

STROM: Oh, that's good. Someone told me recently that you're a great poker player and you've been doing well. Do you have a system?

DIBIASI: Well, you know, Nikki, it's funny you should ask about that, because I've been playing for fifteen years and it's only in the last few years that I've been winning consistently.

STROM: Really? What have you been doing differently?

DIBIASI: Basically, I've been concentrating on counting the cards. And I've learned when to take calculated risks and bluff.

STROM: Do you think learning to take risks in a hobby makes it easier to take risks in other areas?

DIBIASI: Absolutely. It's like learning to dance. Once you feel comfortable doing it, you can do it anywhere.

STROM: That's interesting. I've always wanted to play poker. Now I know why I should!

This conversation is more than just mindless small talk or apple polishing; it's one of those interchanges that link people to help hold an organization together. At the same time, it also helps create a rapport that may one day open the door to new business opportunities with the boss.

STRATEGY

MOST of us face similar situations—whether it's at a cocktail party or in the hall waiting for the elevator—where the capacity for small talk is all-important. And almost everybody has, at one time or another, failed at small talk. Remember the scene in the movie *Big* in which the CEO chastises the too-serious ad exec when she starts talking business with him at the company Christmas party? "Susan," he says, "get a drink!" The audience laughs out of recognition: We've all been in situations where we didn't act appropriately. Of course, we could argue that in work situations we shouldn't have to be concerned with "making nice." But work requires a range of behaviors; only narrow-minded people maintain one role.

Strom has to learn to adjust her behavior to the situation. Otherwise she'll never be promoted, despite her considerable ambition and talent. Her "strictly business" attitude is alienating those around her, who perceive it as hostility and uptightness.

Fortunately for Strom, social skills—as opposed to talent and intelligence—can be acquired. She first needs to stop focusing on how she feels and start thinking about other people's feelings, including those of her subordinates. Strom is inhibited because she is behaving as if the whole world were concentrating on her every move—and it's not.

She is also missing the central purpose of small talk: to build trust and loyalty. Rather than trivial chatter or a way for an employee to curry favor with the boss, small talk actually helps strengthen the bonds between people—always a plus for an organization that depends on teamwork.

Sometimes it will also prompt a kind of revelation: Suddenly a person gains insight into another's thought processes. That insight can help the employee produce work closer to what the employer wants, or it can help the employer better understand how to use the employee.

Strom probably will see small talk in its true light once she begins to practice it. Since she feels most comfortable performing tasks, she might want to consider this party an assignment.

Her homework, then: Research the backgrounds and interests of top managers. If she is familiar with their career paths and hobbies, she'll be able to ask intelligent questions that will impress them. For example, if she finds herself waiting for an elevator with the company president, she can inquire about his involvement with Big Brothers rather than wasting the moment talking about the weather.

And instead of asking a commonplace question ("How long have you been in Big Brothers?"), she should try a more unusual question, like "Has a Big Brother ever given a Little Brother a job?" Such a question would be more likely to spark an interesting conversation that, in turn, could lay the foundation for a future relationship with the president.

Since Strom has trouble taking the initiative, she should think of herself as the host of a party rather than as one of the many guests. Even if she is a stranger in a group where everyone is acquainted, she should begin a conversation.

Once I was the only stranger seated at a table with ten newspaper-publishing giants. They were unusually quiet during the consommé, so I decided to plunge right in and ask about something we all had in common: college. At the time I was writing a book about college and the importance of extracurricular activities to careers, so I invited my dinner mates to share their experiences. Everyone did. The result was a fascinating conversation. My question saved the evening for us all. And, not incidentally, it helped my work become known to high-level employees of the newspaper syndicate that had just contracted me.

The key to chatting successfully with strangers lies in a provocative opening. If you see someone wearing an unusual pin, tie, or ring, ask if there is a story behind it. At a Christmas party, ask the important-looking stranger standing by the bar to tell about the best Christmas party she ever attended. Such questions are almost guaranteed to get a conversation going.

And the questions don't have to be brilliant, either. Everyone likes to tell his or her stories; people are usually so flattered that they won't even notice if a question isn't the smartest or smoothest.

After that, all you need to do is listen carefully, ask for details, and offer a few genuine words of praise.

Learning the gift of gab, of course, takes practice. At first, conversation might seem contrived or awkward. And you may stumble and attempt it at the wrong time. With practice, though, you'll quickly become sensitive to timing. And the benefits will be recognizable immediately—in warm relations with superiors and employees, and in a friendlier, easier work environment.

Male Bonding:
Can You Beat It?

When men are the majority,
their culture rules. But you don't
have to feel like a
foreigner.

After the meeting, corporate real estate senior VP Carol Givens is irritated—at her colleagues and at herself. Her five male peers were up to their usual antics: throwing paper clips, replaying the Redskins game ad nauseam, telling jokes. Finally, fed up, she said, "Let's get down to business. I have a noon meeting." Phil Peters brushed her off, saying, "Lighten up, Carol."

So Givens left feeling like a disciplinarian mother, not a role she relishes. She also felt left out, and she didn't know why. Givens always believed that she could succeed and gain recognition simply through hard work and determination. For the most part, she has. After a decade and a half in the real estate business, she's finally won a salary and perks on a par with the top-ranked males in her firm. But the gap between her fantasy of what inclusion in the top ranks would mean and its reality is beginning to unnerve her.

Givens can't fit in. Her male peers haven't ostracized her or undermined her work. They're democratic in their games—no one is excluded. But while the guys seem to thrive on jokes and pranks, Givens is revolted by them. She doesn't understand their boyish behavior during meetings or their dinners at the Moroccan restaurant with the belly dancers or their weekend golf games. What place can she have with these young and middle-aged old boys?

□ # THE WORDS TO SAY: GETTING DOWN TO BUSINESS WITH THE BOYS □

When men tease each other, it's about power: *Can you one-up me? Are you strong enough to take it?* But when a man teases a woman, she sees it as an attack on her vulnerable spot: *He doesn't think I'm smart enough.* If she accepts the challenge, however, and reasserts her power by teasing him back, she both shuts him up and earns his respect. Givens can't really salvage that last meeting, when Peters brushed her off, but she can prepare herself for similar situations in the future by figuring out what horseplay, teasing, and clowning around really mean to men and women.

Scene: A meeting of Peters, four other men, and Givens. The guys have been tossing paper clips, teasing, joking in between items on the agenda.

GIVENS: Quit fooling around, you guys. We've got to get this proposal in by tomorrow morning.
SHE FEELS: You're behaving like jerks, and it makes me feel like one myself. I'm tired of wasting time and resent

the fact that I'm always the one who has to play mother hen.

PETERS: Oh, right, Carol. I forgot you have your eye on the CEO's chair.

HE FEELS: Teasing means you're one of us. You're strong enough to take it and good enough to warrant my attention. It also says I've got the power.

SHE FEELS: You sound hostile when you tease. You undermine my accomplishments and ambitions, which enrages me. And you tread on my feelings, which hurts.

GIVENS (*laughs and throws a paper clip at him*): I hope your research is better than your throwing arm.

SHE FEELS: Okay, you're acting like a kid, but I'll play your game to assure you that I still like you and am not here to reprimand you. And if I do it well, there's a chance you'll ease up on your antics so we can get something done. I'm putting myself on an equal footing, even though this isn't how I'd conduct a meeting.

HE FEELS: You've played the game and you're one of us. Although I don't appreciate the jab, I respect you for reasserting your power—we're on an equal footing now.

☐ ☐

STRATEGY

WHAT Givens is witnessing is the boys' club. In its extreme state, it's another culture with its own customs. Those rituals seem alien to Givens because she is accustomed to the female culture. Men, more than women, belong to "the group"— whether it's a football team or a college fraternity, an army battalion or a corporate department.

Some call this male bonding. What it's about is belonging.

Belonging in a man's world demands convention. In a woman's world, belonging requires support and caring. The contrasts are remarkable. To understand them, Givens needs to study her male co-workers as if they were subjects in a sociological case—coolly and objectively.

If she can't, she won't make it. True, not all male managers partake in these male rituals. But some will, and they will be quick to label her mom, teacher, cop, goody two-shoes. She'll be called "too sensitive," "hysterical," "premenstrual," or worse. The reality is that if she complains to her peers directly, she won't be understood. They'll call it nagging and dismiss it. That's the catch-22. How can she play their games without feeling that she's selling out? How can she possibly change such an entrenched system?

Givens will do better if she stomachs the innocuous game playing and does not get bogged down in making everything right—that is, in her own image. After all, a man who worked in a mostly female office probably would have to listen to women talking about diets, fashion, and health—topics that aren't typically favorites of men. Givens might not feel so frustrated if she looked at their time-wasting activities as preliminaries that are as intrinsic to the male culture as singing the national anthem at a ball game.

But if too much time is wasted in male posturing, Givens has to make another kind of choice. Rather than take on the system directly, confronting her male co-workers while she is outnumbered, she should try a better strategy: manipulating it—buttonholing one or two of the men before the meeting, asking about their priorities, and sharing her own. In other words, instead of complaining about their poor behavior, which sets her up as the bad guy, she should express what she hopes they can get accomplished. A simple "What's on your plate that's interesting these days?" or "What projects are you working on that I can support?" will do. This approach forces the men to be more responsive to her and her goals, and is more likely to get her what she wants.

That doesn't mean Givens has to sell out. It simply means that to belong she needs to prove herself in terms the men can understand. After all, if they spoke French during these meetings and she knew the language, wouldn't she *parler* in turn? It may not be any more significant than that. Givens might just experiment by reading the sports page in the newspaper for a month and chatting about what she reads. She may find greater bonding in that small, nonwork arena than she could imagine. And certainly she couldn't lose anything by trying.

One last point, however. If Givens has the courage to be an agent of change and has the ear of the CEO or other top players, or if she knows that top management has tried to bring in more women but can't keep them, she might offer an opinion. If she decides to take on this role, she should explain to a sympathetic corporate leader that women feel isolated in the face of male fishing or golf expeditions. And she can point out that an increasing number of progressive companies are taking steps to organize more women-friendly retreats and conferences.

She might cite some of these examples: A decade ago, Avon Products, Inc., changed its annual President's Golf Day, which provided an informal opportunity for executives to socialize with each other, to include tennis and swimming. Not surprisingly, more women executives began to join in. Procter & Gamble and Ethicon, Inc., a subsidiary of Johnson & Johnson, sponsor cultural diversity workshops to help men and women try to understand each other's point of view.

Change is usually quite slow in coming. But the longer Givens is there, the greater will be her contribution to the company, the more women she'll bring in and champion, and the better the odds that eventually she'll leave her mark.

THEY'RE JEALOUS:
WILL IT HURT
YOUR JOB?

*Their weapons are gossip,
snide comments, and subtle
sabotage. Here's how to
protect your turf.*

Gloria Katz never expected to overhear staffers badmouthing her, but that's exactly what happened when she was promoted to manager. *What do you think Gloria had on the top guys? . . . I don't know, but she definitely had something. She certainly didn't earn that promotion. There is no way she should have gotten promoted over you or Mr. . . .*

Suppressing her anger, hurt, and desire to set the record straight, Katz realizes that she is now set apart from her staff. During her three years in the corporate-training division of a multinational company, Katz has advanced rapidly. She has worked hard and deserves her promotion, but she now understands that not all of her colleagues see it that way.

At thirty-four, she is the youngest manager there, supervising not only those who are several years older than she is but also people who have seniority in the company. One of the individuals she heard talking about her has been with the company for twelve years. In addition, it took many other managers who are now her peers as long as five years to secure the promotion that she attained with just eighteen months of direct experience.

Katz has wanted this promotion more than anything else, but she is unprepared for the hostility and resentment it has generated. Lately when she approaches a group of managers, she is often met with silence, which signals to her that they have been talking about her. And snipes from the staff are frequent and sharp. Just this morning, when Katz left a general meeting to retrieve a report she had left on her desk, she overheard one of the staffers "jokingly" remark, "It's a wonder she can find anything on that desk of hers."

These jabs are unnerving, and Katz is not sure how to respond. Part of her wonders whether she isn't somehow to blame: Is she coming off too brash—should she act more solicitous? Or should she become tougher and ignore the slings and sneers of those who resent her success? Or maybe she should just confront her hostile colleagues and address the issue frankly.

☐   THE WORDS TO SAY: ☐
WINNING OVER YOUR
ENEMIES

Katz feels most uncomfortable around another manager, Evelyn Price, who is forty-three years old and has been with the company for twelve years. Price is extremely hostile toward Katz; though she doesn't say why, it's clear she is upset at Katz's fast advancement and feels envious of her.

She realizes that Katz is rising so steadily and so fast that in a few years she may well eclipse Price, who may find herself one of Katz's subordinates. Rather than pretend the jealousy doesn't exist, Katz makes an attempt to defuse Price's anger by showing her that she values her.

KATZ: I just wanted to thank you for your congratulations the other day. It means a lot to me.

PRICE: Well, it really is a coup, you know. No one else here has ever been promoted as fast as you have. It's a tough job. I hope you can prove yourself—for your sake.

KATZ: I hope so, too. I've been thinking a lot about how I'm going to approach my new responsibilities, particularly the affirmative-action program. And I've realized how important support from the other managers in the department, especially you, will be to me. As the newest manager, I know I can really benefit from your insights and expertise in particular. In fact, your help is essential.

PRICE: Well, I really don't know how much time we're going to have for tutoring. We're all very busy, you know. We've all got our own jobs to do.

KATZ: Of course. What I meant is that I'm beginning to see how we all fit together as a team, what we all can offer each other—and the company. It's good to know I can count on you for your support, Evelyn.

□   □

STRATEGY

KATZ is paying one of the hidden costs of success: envy. Few of us think about this negative aspect of succeeding, but nobody can advance without facing it. It is rampant.

Think about it. The media are filled with stories of the downfall of eighties overachievers—and who doesn't see them without secretly feeling some vengeful glee? As the baby boomers age and try to climb the corporate pyramid, competition becomes fiercer and envy becomes epidemic. Fewer and fewer people will be chosen for the plum jobs because there are fewer jobs at the top.

Those who are not chosen inevitably find themselves afflicted with the envy bug. Those who nurse it and turn it into grudges will find that ultimately it is self-destructive and hinders their advancement.

Everybody has felt envy, and everybody has at times become a target of it. For women, though, it can be a particularly unsettling experience. More than men, women are socialized toward the notion of "fair play" and acknowledgement of others' contributions. They have a harder time accepting the separation that achievement brings. Being the star—being set apart as a leader—feels wrong to women. But despite these feelings, Katz hasn't done anything wrong; she should persevere.

Trying to appease the snipers with self-deprecating remarks ("Hey, it's the luck of the draw—you'll be next!") or trying to ingratiate herself with fawning praise will not be productive. She will only come off as insincere or, even worse, confirm views that the promotion is undeserved.

Confrontation, while it seems a direct, honest way of handling the situation, is an even worse approach. That's because what makes envy so troubling to deal with is that it is considered a shameful emotion, one to which few will confess, even to themselves. Rather than admitting they are jealous of the achiever, those who feel envy do what Katz's colleagues and subordinates are doing—they act mean-spirited, invent spurious explanations of her success, and erect a wall that separates the achiever from themselves. Confronting them, asking them for their views, will only give them an opportunity to project their hostility.

So what option does Katz have? First, she has to accept the fact that envy is inevitable and let it run its course. In the meantime, she should remain calm, cool, diplomatic, not betraying her concern over the behavior. If she overhears a nasty comment, she should pretend she did not hear it. If someone says something antagonistic to her face, she should not respond in kind; rather, she should try to defuse the situation with good humor and grace. To their salvo "Do you think you can handle it?" she should respond, "I sure hope so." Showing that she doesn't take herself too seriously and is able to laugh at herself will force others to loosen up.

She should also let her detractors know that she needs their support; that they are all part of a team; that she hopes they can continue to work together; that when the department and division succeed, they will all succeed.

Sound familiar? Recognize the language? It's that company line you used to hear coming from the boss's lips. When you are promoted you need to get used to it coming from your own. Now that you are the boss, you need to accept your role, accept the meanness of former peers, and demand that your employees do their work to the best of their ability. Otherwise, you will have to use your authority and *take measures*. That means warnings, probations, transfers, even firings.

Sound harsh? It's realistic. When it comes right down to it, it's you or them. You have to bet on yourself, vote for yourself, or you will become a weak boss, the kind you never respected. While envy originates with them, it will become a problem only if you allow it to persist. It is up to you to understand that it is *their* problem, and probably will be short-lived.

Katz should remind herself that her own superiors regard her highly; that's why she has advanced rapidly. When she is faced with a difficult staff or peer, she should consider seeking advice from one of her bosses, who undoubtedly have experienced the same rite of passage.

Once you learn to deal with envy in others, you may find it easier to recognize it when you find yourself envious of someone else. For if enduring the envy of others is the price of success, acknowledging your own feelings of envy—no matter how embarrassing—often can be just the whip necessary to motivate yourself to compete harder.

GOSSIP:

WHEN YOU SHOULD

Spreading petty rumors
can hurt your career. Passing
useful information
can help it.

Diane Nugent, an account executive at a large advertising agency, reserved a table for three at Le Bistro, the newest luncheon hot spot for creative bigwigs. Using the excuse of celebrating a break-through in a difficult project, Nugent asked two colleagues to join her for a long lunch of *beignets aux fromages*. Seated amid large portraits of literati and dining from exquisite, handcrafted plates, Nugent was eager to start dishing—not the sumptuous food but the gossip. The three women immediately began their usual round-robin style of swapping stories: who's doing what to whom, and why.

In the middle of "How long do you think the new assistant vice president will last?" Nugent noticed what she immediately identified as a mini-drama taking place at a corner table across the restaurant. Dorothy Adams, senior vice president of a com-peting advertising agency and one of the industry's rising stars, was engaged in a toast with Bill Lester, head of Nugent's company's most important client. "What do you think is going on there?" Nugent asked. Her companions immediately began to speculate. Maybe Adams was leaving her company to work for Lester. Or—their worst fear—perhaps they were losing their biggest account. If so, would that mean they would be laid off?

By the time Nugent got back to the office two hours later, she was absolutely convinced that her company was in fact on the verge of losing its largest account. After all, as one of her colleagues had pointed out, Adams was the type of person who would brazenly steal clients—how else could she have risen so high so fast? "Who knows what kind of things Adams was telling Lester! She can be so sleazy!" another said. Nugent was beside herself with anger and indignation at Adam's conduct, but most of all she was worried about how it would affect the agency.

And so, back at the office after lunch, Nugent stood at Marge Gould's door for several minutes, wondering how she should break the bad news to her boss.

☐ # TELL ALL OR HUSH UP? ☐
A QUIZ

Differentiating between useful information and gossip is difficult. There are no simple rules on when to keep your mouth shut and when to spread the news. Test your understanding of the boundaries—and find out whether you need to change your tactics.

1. *You discover that a co-worker has a conflict of interest in a project she has taken on. You:*
   A. Confront the co-worker and suggest she give the project to someone else.

B. Confide in your boss.

C. Tell colleagues about it.

D. Keep quiet.

ANSWER: A. Direct confrontation is the best approach when you're attempting to stop wrongful behavior. B is risky—it might make you seem like a tattler. C would prove that you are a tattler, and petty to boot. D is cowardly. Belonging to a team means speaking up when it will benefit your company.

2. *Your boss gives all of the plum assignments to one manager. You:*

A. Meet with your boss to explain why she is wrong.

B. Reveal your boss's bias to her boss.

C. Talk to a friend at work about it.

D. Keep quiet.

ANSWER: C. A co-worker may give you insight into your behavior and your boss's. At the least, this will let you release some steam. A is too dangerous and would require consummate grace to pull off. B is riskier, since you may alienate not only your boss but her boss as well. D will add to your resentment.

3. *Your boss asks you not to tell anyone about an ad agency he is considering hiring. You know it could provide a dear friend with a job she desperately needs. You:*

A. Try to convince your boss to reconsider his request for confidentiality.

B. Hint about the possibility with co-workers to see who else knows.

C. Alert your friend and swear her to secrecy.

D. Keep quiet.

ANSWER: D. Sometimes saying nothing is the smartest action you can take. A would require enormous tact and could backfire. B almost certainly would backfire. And as for C, you may think you'd be doing a friend a favor, but leaking information when you know only part of the story is dangerous and foolhardy.

☐   ☐

STRATEGY

AND what exactly is the "bad news"? What did Nugent see? She saw a client and a competitor eating lunch together and toasting each other. So? Two and two don't always make four. Perhaps Lester and Adams are flirting, in which case it's no one's concern (except perhaps their significant others'). Or maybe Adams is thanking Lester for helping her daughter get into his alma mater. Or maybe it's something equally harmless. There are a myriad of different explanations for their lunch, and any one of them could be true.

Nugent is in a difficult spot. Like many of us, she is walking that thin but crucial line between passing information and trading in gossip. It's essential that you know the difference. The latter can get you in big trouble and cause irreparable damage to innocent people, while the former is absolutely necessary to survive in today's competitive environment.

Doing business requires sharing information, especially in advertising and other service industries, where change is a constant. You need to be plugged in to networks so you hear the grapevine information, such as whose accounts are up for grabs and what changes are going on inside your company. Even information like your boss's aversion to long meetings is relevant, for it provides the basis for action.

Gossip, however, is not intended for action; it is intended for status. You reveal something to prove you're "in" so you can be rewarded with secrets that you don't yet know. Gossip, then, is a bribe, a way of enhancing your status at someone else's expense. The information that is revealed can frequently be extremely hurtful. In fact, people often gossip out of a malicious desire for revenge; they're envious or angry, and gossip is their way of striking back. In Nugent's case, I wonder whether jealousy was behind her colleagues' belief that Adams would "brazenly" steal a client. If so, they need to be careful—they may take other steps more vindictive than just badmouthing Adams among themselves, which will almost certainly backfire on them.

Still, the possibility exists that Adams was indeed taking away the company's most important client. For this reason, Nugent needs to tell her boss what she saw—that will make her a good team player. But before she speaks she should remind herself that all she knows is that a client and a competitor toasted each other in a trendy restaurant. Leaking information when you know only part of the story is dangerous. Nugent should proceed cautiously and explain her concerns without engaging in potentially destructive and unfair speculation—in other words, gossip.

Nugent needs to be careful not to allow her talk to turn nasty, not to characterize Adams's business conduct as sleazy. You have to be cognizant of your motives and exercise caution and discretion. You should also keep in mind that the truth, even when searched for diligently, is elusive. (If you have any doubts, just watch the classic film *Rashomon* for a quick study in individual realities.) Another rule of thumb: If you feel bad after a dishing session, then you've probably stepped over the line into gossip.

Of course, we are social creatures and sometimes we will use gossip as a way of bonding with people. Most of the matters we gossip about, from our boss's new diet to a First Lady's alleged peccadilloes, do not have any serious repercussions. And if we speak about people we know in a kind manner and with good intentions, we may actually help them. If you hear your boss is having family problems, you can be extra sensitive, for example.

But the person who blabs rumors unthinkingly can inflict

harm not only on others but on herself, for ultimately few will respect or trust her, and with good reason. However, going to the tight-lipped and aloof opposite extreme will put you outside of the information loop, and no one can afford that. Aim, then, to be the model of prudence and discretion, one who is plugged in to the information pipeline but reveals only what is useful, and only to those who need to know.

ARE YOU
A BAD BOSS?

Your staff won't tell
you how they really feel,
but you can still
find out.

Anne Markle, senior vice president of a large retail organization, is shocked, angry, and hurt. She has just completed an exit interview with one of her employees, Miriam Stoner, who spent the entire forty-five minutes dispassionately explaining why she has hated working for Markle. First among Stoner's grievances was that Markle gave unclear directions, which the staff had to spend hours trying to decipher. Second, she said that no matter what kind of work was produced, Markle was not satisfied and would demand senseless changes. Stoner said that it was as if Markle wanted to remind everyone that she was the boss and they were the peons. Third, Markle pretended to be everyone's friend but then would assert her rank or use people's confidences to further her own agenda.

Markle's first reaction was to dismiss Stoner's complaints as sour grapes. After all, she had denied Stoner's request for a promotion only six months earlier. But for all of Stoner's flaws, she was not irrational or given to hyperbole. It seemed out of character for her to invent charges.

Markle felt herself react strongly to Stoner's objections. She was especially wounded by the charge that she proffered false friendship. She had always prided herself on being an accessible, humane, and considerate boss, chatting with her staff because she was genuinely interested in their lives, not out of a hidden Machiavellian motive. When Markle became a manager three years ago, she vowed that she would never be like the awful bosses she had worked for. But now she is facing the rather unpleasant possibility that she has become exactly what she has always hated—a bad boss.

☐ # EVERYTHING YOU ALWAYS WANTED TO KNOW . . . ☐

If your company doesn't have a formal management-assessment program and you have a staff of more than three, you can institute your own. Hold a meeting in which you discuss the need to hear an honest appraisal of your skills. Then ask your staff to respond—anonymously, of course—to the following questionnaire. The results will provide you with the information you need.

1. Are my directions usually clear, or do you depend on your co-workers to help you figure out what your tasks are?
2. Do I often change my mind and alter your assignments after you've already begun them?
3. Do I usually edit your work without improving it?
4. Am I usually open to new ideas and innovative plans?
5. Do you think that I am disappointed in your work?

6. Do I provide constructive criticism?
7. Do you trust me?
8. Do I help develop your skills and promote you?
9. Am I available to you when you need additional assistance?
10. Do I create or operate in a crisis mode too often?

STRATEGY

BEFORE Markle can figure out whether or not she is a bad boss, she needs to understand what a good one is. Recognizing that her greatest asset is a hard-working, enthusiastic staff, a good boss encourages, develops, and promotes her employees. One way she does this is by accepting—even encouraging—criticism and then learning from it. She recognizes that subordinates' gripes should be treated as seriously as supervisors' complaints. As a result, a good boss's office is much more likely to run efficiently, productively, and profitably.

Markle is lucky. She has gotten a red flag that her performance is falling short. Most employees won't risk giving their bosses uninvited critiques. Consequently managers need to initiate the assessment process themselves. In Markle's case, she already knows that she needs to investigate whether the staff shares Stoner's opinion of her. But whether there is a warning signal or not, every supervisor needs to find out if she is an effective manager. And if she finds out she isn't, she then needs to modify her management style.

So how do you assess yourself? The first, most obvious way to learn how you're doing is to ask your employees for feedback. Hold private, one-on-one performance-review sessions with each member of your staff. Simple enough, but few managers bother to do it, thinking either that no one would tell them the truth or that they already know how they're doing. They're dead wrong.

Employees appreciate the chance to air their grievances. You just need to ask them the right questions in the right way. If you ask, "What do you think of me?" you aren't likely to hear anything but praise. But they will likely respond frankly to questions that don't require them to directly assess your abilities, such as "How can I help you perform your job better and achieve our goals?" Some other good questions: "What do you wish I did differently?" and "What other tasks would you like me to undertake?"

During these sessions, you will have to be an active listener. Ask for specific examples, and paraphrase what has been said to make sure you understand. While these sessions will undoubtedly be difficult, they will provide you with a great deal of information.

Next, consider using the criticism you hear in private sessions at staff meetings. For example, if your employees accuse you of being dictatorial or preemptory, ask them to suggest alternatives to plans that you have proposed. Also, pay close attention to the nonverbal signs your staff communicates. Do your employees always agree with you? Do they seem comfortable speaking up, or do they seem cowed in your presence?

Assuming that Markle does discover in one-on-one meetings that Stoner's complaints are shared by others, she needs to ask a few pointed questions to make sure her instructions are absolutely clear when she gives them. Is there anything that needs to be clarified? Has anything been left out of her instructions? Since she has been accused of being hypercritical, she should monitor her reaction closely and take pains not to lay blame.

Perhaps most important for any boss who wants to assess her performance, Markle needs to closely examine her underlying motives and insecurities. Why did she feel especially hurt by Stoner's charge that she offers false friendship? Why did that complaint sting more than the others? Had someone accused Markle of this before? Often we feel a pang when we are faced with a painful truth about ourselves.

Markle also needs to ask herself whether there is a pattern to her alleged flaws. It seems to me that Stoner's three complaints could all easily stem from a manager's feelings of inadequacy. Managers often give muddled assignments and unclear directions not because they want to confuse their staffs (as some manipulative bosses might) but because they're too overwhelmed or too afraid to think through their plans. Similarly, they are excessively critical because they need to focus on their staff members' weaknesses in order to feel strong.

As for Markle's best-friend act, I've noticed that many new managers, especially women, seem to have difficulty assuming the distance required of a manager. They feel uncomfortable being the authority figure and don't understand the difference between being liked and being a good manager. A good manager isn't a buddy or a confidante; she is a mentor, motivator, and leader.

By periodically playing the scolding schoolmarm, Markle falls into the trap of making her staff into bad kids so that she can then call them to order and punish them. This, in turn, causes her to fail at her real role: furthering her department's economic vitality by enabling her staff to be as productive as possible.

Interesting developments occur when an organization is willing to examine management styles. At Monsanto, for example, employee advocacy manager Jennifer Luner recently launched a program to encourage feedback between employees and their bosses. Using a list of undesirable and desirable traits (such as "rarely lets anyone know how they are doing" and "provides feedback on work performance"), employees were asked to rate their managers. Then each employee passed on this assignment to his or her manager's boss. It was there that Luner discovered a curious syndrome: Those behaviors that employees disliked— such as insensitivity—were apparent also in upper management. Conversely, a commitment from the very top can make an effective management style a reality.

At Monsanto, each manager meets with his or her superior to discuss an employee's evaluation. It's up to the manager to figure out how to improve his or her relationship with the employee. But six months later the questionnaire is distributed again, and the supervisor expects to see a change.

Unfortunately many companies do not have a formal management-assessment program. But you don't need the backing of your company. Bosses who want to inspire their staffs and enable them to realize their potential take it upon themselves to be evaluated, because they recognize that it is essential to becoming a successful manager.

Enemies:

A Career Story

Part of professional
development lies in protecting
yourself from ill will.

"The conclusions don't add up. You're out in left field again, Princess," sneered Bob Walters, a marketing analyst at the bank. Eleanor King, also a marketing analyst, sat in embarrassed silence as the rest of the staff—fifteen senior analysts and one director— erupted in giggles at Walters's demeaning nickname for King.

King was convinced that Walters had deliberately misinterpreted her report, but this attack—*out in left field again, Princess*— and the others' laughter blindsided her and left her unable to defend herself. When the two-hour meeting ended, she watched Walters, obviously pleased with himself, waltz out with the director, Mr. Beasley, chatting and laughing.

Later she confronted Walters, asking him why he was so hostile to her. He denied doing anything wrong and told her, "You're being hypersensitive. What's the matter? Having trouble with Mr. King?"

King has been hoping that people would see through Walters, but the meeting proved that they haven't. What's worse, Walters has become her aggressive enemy in a war he started and seems intent on winning. She doesn't know why. At the age of thirty-eight, she has never had an enemy before, at least not since she was a child at war with her older sister.

How did she get into this predicament?

The two analysts were hired as equals two years ago. Walters has always jockeyed for position, but in the last few months he has seemed to do so at King's expense. He extends a courtly manner toward the department staff, regularly praising their efforts, complimenting their style, and soliciting their advice. But to King, his only peer, he is critical and sarcastic in public; in private, he is dismissive or malicious. At meetings he points out defects in her proposals and mocks her.

At first she thought if she ignored him he would eventually become bored with his antics. But her lack of reaction seemed only to intensify his efforts. So she tried to be understanding of Walters, even though his behavior was hopelessly immature. She tried to forgive him and treat him as an injured friend, but he lashed out at her for being holier-than-thou.

A friend has suggested that she fight back—"beat him at his own game." But the irony is that King's belief in herself, which Walters denigrates as self-righteousness, prevents her from engaging in dirty politics. She knows she must act to save the situation, but she doesn't know how.

☐ TEN WAYS TO NEUTRALIZE ☐ YOUR NEMESIS

Handling an enemy requires finesse, strength, and determination. Here are some tactics:

1. Analyze the conflict, and admit your role in it. Is there some way in which you are adding to the hostility?

2. Laugh away an insult with a comment such as "Lighten up!"

3. Fight back publicly. Defend the merits of your concept or program, and tell your nemesis that you'd be willing to explain it more thoroughly after the meeting.

4. Kill him with kindness. Do him an enormous favor to upset the scales. Get him a hard-to-get ticket to a big game or theater event. Help his child get into your alma mater by writing a compelling letter of recommendation. Your enemy will then owe you.

5. Get to know him. Find out how he got the job, who his mentors are, what his motives and goals are. Knowledge is power.

6. Build up your own troops to outnumber the enemy's. Make sure that some top managers are included in your camp. Numbers count.

7. Confront him. Demand that he treat you with respect.

8. Stay visible. Keep producing work. Contribute innovative concepts and let people know about your accomplishments.

9. Get rid of your enemy. Find him another, perhaps even better job through your own grapevine of headhunters and colleagues. Some people have even sent their nemeses' résumés to blind ads in a newspaper or a trade journal.

10. Develop your networks. If all else fails, you'll need to find a new job.

STRATEGY

LEARNING to deal with an enemy is one of those career skills you need on order to thrive. King doesn't want to hear that. Many women don't. Why? As I've said before, women are conditioned to want life to be "nice." Women want everyone to feel liked, even loved as well as respected. We want to avoid conflicts, where feelings may be hurt, so we try to make sure even our enemy feels good, sometimes neglecting ourselves in the process.

But no matter how cordial and accommodating you are, as you advance you will encounter enemies, people who want exactly what you want and don't want you to have it. Part of professional development lies in acknowledging and protecting yourself against the animosity.

Before King can conquer her foe, she needs to analyze the dynamic between Walters and herself and learn from it. The first step is in recognizing that neither of them is entirely "right." Most feuds are not a matter of good *versus* evil. In all likelihood, both King and Walters are contributing to their bad relationship. When dealing with an office nemesis, you need to ask: What do the two of us despise about each other, and why?

Competition is a prime breeder of enmity, and competition is fierce these days, as companies are frantically downsizing and the number of middle-level managers vying for the top spots is increasing. But there are other causes. Sometimes people are pulled into the larger office dynamic; for instance, you may have responsibilities that require you to force your co-worker to adhere to strict deadlines, and she may resent you simply for doing your job. Perhaps you are behaving deferentially, and your foe is acting accordingly. Or you may seem dismissive of his knowledge and, ego bruised, he lashes back in anger. Finally, it could be that you both dislike in each other what you see and dislike in yourselves.

In King's case, competition is clearly at the root of the animosity. Walters is obsessed with being the favorite son and does not want to share anything—position, access, or favor—with his peer. To capture the limelight, he is willing to bully, connive, and lie. On King's end, she is failing to resist Walters's behavior. In fact, she is encouraging it.

King's initial strategy was to deny that the animosity existed. That only fanned Walters's hatred. Ignoring the enemy makes you an easy target; it may embolden him to intensify his attacks, as it did in King's case.

Her second response was to assume a superior stance; Walters, she reasoned, was in need of her understanding. Walters correctly interpreted this as self-righteousness and became even angrier.

King needs to ask herself why she dreads confronting Walters. (She tried talking to him but gave up too easily.) Is she reliving some past experience—a sibling rivalry, perhaps—allowing Walters, the stronger, to win, as her previous foe did? The fact that King, a veteran professional, his risen as far as she has without encountering an emeny is remarkable and, in some ways, unfortunate. For now, at thirty-eight, she is facing perhaps the single most important challenge of her career: the need to fight for herself.

Instead of asking Walters to treat her better, she should demand it: "I have been analyzing your hostility toward me for the past few months, and I am confused by it. I have tried to be a supporter of yours from the beginning, but it seems you have become progressively more vicious to me. We need to deal with it now." If he refuses, then she has to make it clear that she will not tolerate his disrespectful behavior: "I want you to drop these attacks. We're a team here, and there is no room for this kind of behavior."

Each time Walters criticizes her publicly, she must respond, whether with a stern word or a half-serious joke. At the last meeting, for example, when Walters accused her of being off base, she might have replied, "My conclusions aren't off-the-wall. In fact, I'll show you in detail after this meeting if you'd like. While you may disagree with my thinking, I assure you that you will find my work is valid." That allows her to save face and forces the staff to recognize his venom.

All too often people witness such strife but, not knowing how to handle it, do nothing and therefore appear to be sanctioning the act. King must train herself to be stronger; she will find that, as a result, others will become stronger supporters of her. She might also reach out to peers and superiors, asking them about how they have handled similar situations.

But under no circumstances should she complain to her boss. No manager wants to have employees gripe about a dilemma without posing a solution, nor does a manager want to hear that employees are not getting along. In fact, King does not know Beasley's view of the situation. He may see through Walters's game but be waiting it out, or perhaps he covertly enjoys the spectacle of his underlings vying for his approval. What is critical now is that King not let Walters drive her away from Beasley or anyone else. To hide is to lose.

King will probably never make Walters her friend, but if she starts to flex her muscles, she'll soon know whether she has defused the situation or needs to request a transfer or find another job. In the meantime, the experience can transform her into a strong, more confident professional who is able to protect herself in any situation.

SUBTLE
SEXISM

It may be less
blatant, but it can
be just as devastating to
your career.

Joan Wilson, an in-house attorney with an aerospace company, was stunned. At a morning meeting, a colleague, John Dunham, had proposed that the legal department develop a checklist for employees taking depositions to ensure more thorough sessions, and he was hailed as a genius. Wilson had pitched the same idea just one month ago, and it was dismissed. "Too much work," said Bob Griffin, a fellow attorney, who now called Dunham's plan "brilliant." No one even glanced at Wilson to check her reaction. Had they really forgotten that she had proposed the idea? Was she considered that much of a nonentity?

When Wilson was hired sixteen months ago, she heard a lot of talk about being a team player. She has tried to become one, but as one of only two woman lawyers in the twenty-five person legal department, she has continually felt unwanted, even invisible. To say her company is male-dominated would be an understatement. Only three professional women in the entire

163

corporation can reserve a seat in their own names in the executive dining room. When Wilson is invited to lunch with her peers, the conversation inevitably turns to endless sports talk or crude jokes. At industry functions, colleagues frequently "forget" to introduce her or exclude her from conversations. Their office conduct is equally reprehensible. At meetings, she finds her ideas are ignored, or stolen. Even some of her own staff disregard her, discussing projects with other colleagues instead.

Should she complain to her boss? Wilson wants to change the situation, but many of her women friends at other aerospace companies complain of similar treatment, and they all think there is nothing anyone can do about it. "We just have to wait till there are more women in charge," one friend said. Does Wilson really have to wait that long?

☐ TWELVE WAYS TO SHUT ☐ UP A SEXIST

Those who want to change must make it happen. The next time you're confronted with demeaning behavior, you need to fight back—without alienating anyone. Here's how to do it:

1. *After a crude joke:*

- Say, "Why did you tell that to me?" or, "I haven't heard a joke like that since I was in college."
- Join in and tell a joke of your own.
- Without saying why, excuse yourself for a brief, but noticeable, period of time.

2. *When you're not introduced:*

- Extend your hand and do it yourself.
- Assume the role of leader: "Now that you all know each other, we can proceed. I'm Jane Doe."

- Before a meeting, ask the offending manager how he wants to structure it and say you prefer to introduce yourself.

3. *When your idea is credited to someone else:*

- Say, "I'm sure that Bob could have come up with that plan himself, but actually it was my idea."
- Say, "We're all working so closely together that we may be forgetting what's already been discussed. I brought that idea up last month."
- Say, "Actually, you should be addressing me. I wrote the original proposal."

4. *When staffers express surprise that your work is good:*

- Thank them for noticing.
- Say, "I appreciate your praise. Jim hires only the best lawyers."
- Say, "Good. Now I suggest that we let the firm [or client or competition] know just how good it is."

STRATEGY

THE blatant and harsh sexism of the 1950s and 1960s is mostly gone, and the Archie Bunker–style chauvinists who openly discriminated against women are no longer welcome in most corporations. But women now have to deal with a new kind of sexism. It's subtle with a benign face, but it can be just as devastating to a career, in part because it's so insidious and difficult to prove.

Whether legal or illegal, sexism is always rooted in false expectations. Men expect to enjoy certain privileges. They are conditioned to believe that they will succeed and that women will help and support them—or at least not compete with them. But the landscape has changed. Women are swelling the ranks of middle management (they now make up over 40 percent, according to the U.S. Bureau of Labor Statistics) and are moving into the upper echelons as well. Men are being forced to vie for a shrinking number of positions in companies. Men aren't prepared to see women succeed, especially at their expense. Out of a fear of losing their clients and their jobs, they fight back by telling sophomoric jokes, talking about sports, conveniently forgetting to invite women to lunches, and even stealing ideas.

Note, however, that none of these acts is illegal. No EEOC regulations have been broken, and there are no grounds for a civil suit. But a violation has been experienced, and a career has been damaged. That is what makes subtle sexism so difficult, though not impossible, to combat.

Wilson's friends are wrong; women do not have to wait until there is a significant increase in the number of females in top management. (They also aren't realistic, since a recent study by Catalyst, a New York research organization, found that less than 3 percent of senior managers in the Fortune 500 are women.) There are ways to challenge this tyranny now. First, you need to distinguish between annoying but essentially harmless sexist conduct, such as bad jokes and behavior that are both irritating and harmful, such as not crediting ideas. The former you can choose to fight. The latter you must.

Wilson needs to speak up for herself the moment she hears someone else uttering her idea, especially if it's in a meeting with her co-workers. She needs to send a clear message that no one can take what is hers. Although Wilson's problems stem from the fact that her colleagues are insensitive and lock her out, she is compounding the problem by avoiding confrontation. I've noticed that many women who are victims of discrimination act similarly. They are afraid of doing or saying anything that would antagonize the powers that be, but by keeping silent they allow themselves to be deemed unimportant.

But you can fight back without being belligerent. Wilson, for instance, might have complimented Dunham for his good sense and said she's glad he found her plan useful. She also could have made a joke about copyrighting good ideas. Or she could simply have said, "Actually you should be addressing me. I wrote the original proposal." When her peers neglect to introduce her, she should extend her hand and do it herself. And if they don't invite her to a lunch or a golf game? She should assume the role of scheduler and organize and outing of her own. Initially it will be difficult for her to insinuate herself into their "team," but if she waits for an invitation, she may wait forever.

Wilson also should not tolerate staffers or colleagues who undermine her authority by inviting her employees to discuss their projects with them. Instead of complaining to her boss about their usurping her authority, she first needs to talk to the offending parties. She might arrange a meeting with such a colleague on some other pretext and then casually mention that she wishes he wouldn't provide an audience for her staff. She could say that she knows he is busy and that it is *her* job to handle their questions. Only a fool wouldn't understand her point—and respect her for making it. She can reinforce it by telling her staff that she is always available to talk.

As for distasteful jokes, Wilson is not alone in finding them offensive. When I asked a group of businesswomen whether they like the jokes men tell at work and whether they ever repeat them to their friends, every single one of them said no to both questions. What's the solution? Some women ignore them, recognizing that the jokes really won't damage their careers. Others try to turn the tables on the men and tell equally scatological jokes. Or they simply excuse themselves from the room and hope the men get the message. Whatever you choose to do, don't lecture. You'll only come off as humorless and defensive.

And what about sports talk? Women need to accept the fact that most men are interested in sports, whether we label it as sublimation or not. Because women and men have to work together, women might attempt to bridge this gap. Try an experiment: For one or two months, read the sports pages daily, then join in the conversations. You may discover that you feel more a part of the group and that you are treated as such.

But I can already hear some of you protesting, "Why should *I* change?" The sad fact is that until there are more women in power or more courageous male leaders, it's up to women to figure out ways to succeed in male environments. A rule of thumb: Do battle when most confident of winning and when most in need of the victory. Women are never going to stop men from caring about sports, or maybe even from telling crude jokes, but they can—and must—get men to treat them with respect.

Learning to Compete with Women

> You want to win,
> but not to fight dirty.
> Here's a game plan you
> can live with.

Until recently, Pam Clark considered herself lucky. One of four women in a multinational bank's corporate division, Clark saw her department as a shelter from the harsh, bottom-line atmosphere that dominated the rest of the bank. For the five years she had been with the firm, the women in her unit had worked together as a team. They shared information freely and took pride in each other's successes.

Then the department's director left. A few weeks later the head of her unit, Evelyn Collins, was promoted to vice president of corporate communications. Clark immediately applied for Collins's spot, as did her co-worker Suzanne London, who happens to be one of Clark's closest friends. Since then, there has been a growing distance between them. Where once they discussed everything over a morning cup of coffee, they now only exchange pleasantries, if they talk at all. As far as Clark is concerned, the shift is due solely to London's new attitude, which has become secretive and evasive. Just last week, when Clark asked London what ideas she had for a new project that London was going to be working on, her friend brushed her off, saying, "I haven't really thought much about it yet." The next day Clark heard that London had turned in a three-page memo to Collins on the subject.

Of course, Clark knows they both must lobby their hardest for the position. She expects London to show off her talents, and before London began behaving so shabbily, she even hoped that if she didn't get the promotion, London would. No more.

Does winning a top job require becoming cutthroat? Clark feels confident that she has the experience and talent to handle the position. All she has to do is campaign. But she wonders if she has the stomach to do what is necessary.

☐ SIX WAYS TO MAKE IT ☐ EASIER

Some women find it difficult to compete with other women, particularly their friends. But keeping these ideas in mind can help you deal with the sticky situations (and your own ambivalence):

- Acknowledge your competitive instinct. In the office, attaining your professional goals must be a top priority. Being as creative and productive as you can be will profoundly affect your happiness.
- If you think that senior management will automatically notice and reward you for your excellent work alone, think again. Few see what doesn't stand out.
- Recognize that your loyalties will shift if you decide to go after a job that your boss vacates. Now your focus will be on getting the promotion, not remaining a part of the group, no matter how nurturing it was.

- Emphasize your talents and experience rather than your competitor's failings when lobbying for a promotion or new responsibility. Playing fair will help enhance your reputation in the long run.
- If you find yourself resenting a rival, examine why before considering approaching her. Are you envious of her ability to promote herself? If so, don't fault her—learn from her.
- Separate the professional from the personal in office friendships. Some people may dislike you because you've competed successfully. Keep in mind that at work it's more important to be respected than to be liked.

☐   ☐

STRATEGY

COMPETITION fuels business and egos, and the desire to win becomes keener as you go higher, because the number of job slots decreases. Although women have always competed in the workplace—and, over the last twenty-five years, increasingly against one another—many continue to find it difficult. As with any game, competition comes most easily to those who created the system, set the rules, and were trained to win—in this case, men.

The mere mention of the word *competition* often elicits denial from women. "I'm not really very competitive," many of my clients say. And even those who boast of their ability to play the game become evasive when the subject of competition between women arises. It's no wonder. Feminist experts—from Deborah Tannen, author of the best-selling *You Just Don't Understand*, to scholars such as Carol Gilligan and Nancy Chodorow—have long documented that men are raised to compete and women are taught to be cooperative.

"Masculinity is defined through separation, while femininity is defined by attachment," Gilligan has said. The socialization process begins early: One study of more than 2,400 students from grades 2 through 12 found that boys at all ages were more enthusiastic about competition than were girls who valued collaboration instead. Psychologists such as Gilligan have attributed the difference to the fact that most people are raised primarily by their mothers. In order to develop a male identity, boys have to separate psychologically from their mothers at an early age, whereas girls tend to maintain the connection. Consequently, for women, emotional independence—especially from other females—can be frightening because it seems isolating; for men, it seems natural.

Additionally, experts point out the importance of childhood games. Boys are encouraged through team sports to compete, which teaches them to establish hierarchies, strategize for advantage, and live by the dictum "May be the best man win." But until the women's movement took hold in the seventies, most girls' extracurricular activities consisted primarily of playing with dolls or girlfriends. Through these friendships, girls learn the art of building consensus and forging connections, but they also learn to suppress their competitive instincts, judging them as insensitive, divisive, and unfair. While their propensity for collaboration can make them superior managers, avoiding competition, particularly with other women, can prevent women from getting ahead at work.

Of course, not all women have this fear, and not all men know how to compete fairly. But many women, like Clark, fall into the peculiarly female trap of confusing the professional with the personal. Clark feels as though London has betrayed her because she is keeping her ideas to herself and trying to stand out from the other job candidates. She is angry at her for not being forthcoming about her plan for the new project. But Clark shouldn't have pressed London for that information or expected to get it. Right now London is doing her best to get the job, just as Clark should be doing *her* best. If their friendship collapses, it will be because Clark is demanding a loyalty from London to which she has no right.

Clark is confident of her own talents, and I don't doubt them. What she lacks, though, is the courage to risk winning, because winning will entail giving up being one of the gang and standing alone. If she is promoted, her relationships with London and her current set of peers will inevitably change; she will have to assume a distance. Learning to compete is just one step in the separation process.

Clark first needs to acknowledge and promote her own competitive desires. She wants the job; she should make getting it a priority, just as London has. Will Clark have to resort to backstabbing and dirty dealings in order to get it? Of course not. Anyone who has participated in team sports knows that the goal is not simply to win but to win by playing by the rules.

I have found that my most successful clients understand this implicitly. They build friendships but know when to share information and when to withhold it, when to help others up the ladder and when to look out for themselves. Many of them remain aloof from their rivals so they can see them as the other team and thus campaign harder. They aren't deceitful, but rather are zealously protective of their interests. In short, they have fulfilled their ambitions without causing others harm.

At the other end of the spectrum, there are always those who believe the end justifies the means. I've seen men ruthlessly set out to destroy others' reputations. I've also seen women who are so uncomfortable competing that they turn it into a personal rivalry and launch character attacks. They try to convince themselves—and everyone else—that their colleague is unethical, immoral, or incompetent. Clark has come perilously close to such behavior when she suggests London lacks integrity.

Will Clark feel disloyal acting on her own behalf? At first she will, and some may resent her for it, just as she resents London. In the end, only one person can win the promotion, and moving up often means moving out of a circle of friends.

Advancement often brings loneliness and insularity, and Clark should be aware of that.

If London gets the job, Clark should follow the lead of the professional competitors—athletes—and gracefully accept defeat. In fact, she ought to convey to London her initial sentiment that since she didn't get the promotion, she was glad London did. Will it be difficult? Absolutely. But not to compete would be to lose herself and her chance to contribute. In this regard, it's exactly the same game for men and for women.

LIVING

UP TO GREAT

EXPECTATIONS

> You don't have to
> be perfect—you just have
> to play to your
> strengths.

Paula Morrison, a partner at a large law firm specializing in personal-injury cases, was initially flattered to be chosen as Stewart Powell's replacement when he retired. Then the trouble began.

Ever since she took over his caseload six weeks ago, people have been comparing Morrison with Powell—unfavorably. *Powell always got rid of depositions in a few days . . . Too bad Powell isn't on the case. He could help us out here . . . You had to settle? Powell would have taken them on—and buried them.*

The firm's longtime superstar, Powell was one of those legal giants next to whom everyone else seems small. In thirty years of practice, he rarely lost a case and was so revered that no one addressed him by his first name. At office meetings he was the center of attention, charming everyone with his jokes and his legal "misadventures," as he called them. Powell was so well liked he was considered flawless.

And that, Morrison has learned, is the problem.

"Powell was human, too!" Morrison wants to shout. In the last few weeks, in fact, she has discovered just *how* human. Sure, he was a talented litigator, but he often let details slide that ended up costing the firm time and money. (Powell would sometimes forget to direct the associates to file court briefs in some of his smaller and less glamorous cases.)

Powell also did little to increase the firm's client base. Morrison has brought in more clients in her seven years with the firm than Powell did in thirty. In addition, she is working on a plan to expand the firm's bankruptcy practice; if she's successful, it could triple their billable hours in just a few years.

Morrison knows she won't ever be the master litigator Powell was. Few could be. She had hoped, though, that her accomplishments might compensate for this. Now she fears that she can't deliver what the firm wants. "Don't worry," a partner told her when she voiced her concerns. "We know you can do the job."

But she is beginning to wonder whether the partners really do believe that. She is tempted to tell them the truth about Powell's shortcomings. Or should she try to show his deficiencies by stressing her strengths in those areas? She wonders whether there is any way to satisfy the partners. Is she simply in over her head?

STRATEGY

THE fear of not measuring up is common. It can arise not only when you're expected to fill someone else's big shoes, but also when you start a new job, have demanding bosses, or simply feel in over your head. In all these cases, you may feel tremendous pressure to live up to the standards set by a predecessor, your bosses, or yourself. And often there are serious consequences involved in not fulfilling those expectations. Your reputation and self-esteem can be damaged. You can even lose your job.

Women often suffer more in such situations, not because

people expect too much of them, but because they expect too little. Men are assumed to be competent and tend to be given the benefit of the doubt. Women aren't. They are supposed to be dogged do-gooders, not brave new leaders. As a result, women often fade into the background and play the role of helpmeet, while men are encouraged to highlight their assets and become leaders.

This is certainly the case with Powell and Morrison. I have no doubt that Morrison's assessment of Powell is accurate. I've seen many men who have gotten their colleagues to overlook their flaws by playing up their strengths. But there is absolutely nothing wrong with that. In fact, it is exactly what Morrison needs to do.

How? First she needs to deflect the too-often thoughtless comparisons made between her and Powell. Remaining silent is serving only to validate them. It may also be undermining her self-confidence. (Even the strongest person will begin to believe criticism if she hears enough of it.)

But fighting back must be done tactfully. She must not denigrate Powell. That would only make her look petty and would probably alienate her colleagues; no one wants to lose a hero. Instead, she should acknowledge Powell's assets—"Yes, he was a brilliant litigator"—then deftly turn the conversation back to herself: "And I hope that my plan to beef up our bankruptcy practice will benefit the firm as much as his work did. My early estimates show that it could triple our billable hours by the end of '96." By using this strategy, she will send a message to colleagues (and herself) that she has the job under control and doesn't appreciate the comparisons.

Morrison also needs to take strong steps that will make her colleagues focus on her talents. That doesn't mean becoming Powell's mirror opposite, however. The only way to make co-workers and supervisors recognize your true worth is to develop your own vision and style.

Morrison is already working on an innovative and potentially lucrative plan for the company. What she needs to do is promote it. Too often, women shy away from taking center stage and leave it to men like Powell, who are only too eager to grab the spotlight. As soon as she finishes the plan, she might consider organizing a special meeting for the express purpose of unveiling the plan to staff and partners.

Morrison should also consider soliciting Powell's support. I know of one woman who arranged a dinner for her departing boss so she could establish a rapport. The supervisor was flattered by the attention and thus was delighted to have her pick his brain. Morrison might do the same and use the opportunity to deliver a brief speech celebrating Powell's work. By referring to herself as "Powell's successor" and speaking of the tradition in which she hopes to follow, she would not only develop a relationship with him but would also reinforce that she is his equal.

But Morrison needs to be patient. It may take a while before people stop comparing her with Powell. Until then, she might shore up her confidence by reminding herself that, as she was promoted to the position in the first place, *somebody* must think she is a worthy successor. She might even seek out that partner for advice.

And what if she really *is* in over her head? Then she should do what Powell (and most other men) would do—learn the job to the best of her ability. She needs to remember that she doesn't have to be a wunderkind to be appreciated. All she has to do is be confident enough to play up her strengths.

GETTING PERSONAL

> When to talk about your personal problems—and what to say when you do.

Dorothy Watson is upset and worried that it shows. For years Watson, an assistant vice president of advertising for a multi-national manufacturer, managed to keep her marital problems a secret from her colleagues. She and her husband would fight bitterly, but no matter what happened in her troubled home, she was able to put it behind her when she came to work. Now with her marriage of eight years crumbling and her divorce threatening to become ugly and protracted, Watson is finding herself less and less able to maintain a cool professional demeanor. And she is afraid that her colleagues are beginning to notice.

Last week her boss, Jack Holt, snapped at her after she bungled a presentation before him and the firm's CFO: "Next time come prepared!" Watson was supposed to deliver a brief report on advertising revenue projections, but minutes before the meeting, her attorney called with the bad news that her husband had rejected her settlement offer. She was devastated—this meant a whole new round of draining, expensive negotiations. She wanted to cancel the meeting, but what could she say to Holt? That her husband was tormenting her and she could no longer be counted on professionally?

Holt is "a stiff-upper-lip kind of guy"; to him, bringing your troubles into the office is a sign of weakness. Personal problems are supposed to be, well, personal. Holt himself didn't tell a single person at work when his own son was afflicted with Hodgkin's disease. (Watson heard of it accidentally, from a friend who happened to know Holt's wife.) In fact, the only person in the department who is open about her personal problems suffers dearly for it. Single and unhappy about it, Vickey Howe often talks about her boyfriend problems to people at work, and behind her back people laugh at her. Holt is openly disdainful of her, saying to others, "What's Vickey's melodrama of the week?"

Until now, Watson looked down on Howe, too. Early in her career she learned that you should never let personal matters interfere with work. That is why she is so distraught at her own inability to cope. She worries that her work will continue to suffer as her divorce proceeds. She wants to say something so that people will at least understand her erratic behavior. But if she does speak openly, won't her reputation suffer?

STRATEGY

NO matter how reserved, discreet, or well-balanced you are, at some time or another your personal life will intrude on your work. Whether it's a divorce, a relative's illness, or your husband's job loss, you will have a personal crisis that will make it difficult for you to do your job as well as you normally can. How you handle such situations—whether you open up, and to whom and when— is a critical question that can have a profound impact on your reputation, your career, and your private life.

Watson is right to be cautious. The sad fact is that at many companies being open about your problems, while perhaps personally cathartic, can be professionally disastrous. Colleagues might feel resentful that you are dumping on them, or they might see you as needy, unreliable, and therefore unprofessional. To gauge how much to say and when to say it, you must read and follow the cues at your office. The answer lies in the mores of your company, your bosses' attitudes, and the nature of your personal problems.

Take Watson. She knows far more than she thinks she does. She has already intuited that Holt is uncomfortable around those who express their emotions and that her office is inhospitable to open discussions of one's personal life. She sees how scornful Holt is of Howe's openness about her personal life and how Holt himself behaves. After all, he is the stiff-upper-lip kind of guy, who didn't even tell anyone that his own son had a life-threatening disease. Others in her office follow suit. And so should she.

But that doesn't mean she should pretend that nothing is wrong. In fact, while that strategy might work for someone as reserved as Holt, it would undoubtedly backfire for Watson. Like it or not, a life crisis such as divorce does take a toll. Emotional havoc is inevitable. As Watson herself notes, her emotions are beginning to seep out, and Holt is starting to notice that her performance is lagging. If Watson says nothing, her colleagues will probably find out about the divorce anyway, or they will draw their own conclusions, which may be more unfavorable than letting them know the truth.

I know of one woman, for instance, who became insolent after her superiors said they wouldn't consider her repeated requests for a raise after several months. Naturally, her bosses felt that she was being unreasonable, even immature. The fact was that she needed the money for fertility treatments, and every month counted. If her bosses had known that, they might have arranged for an earlier salary review because she was so valuable an employee. But just as important, they would have had a rational explanation for her behavior.

Often the best solution is to speak candidly—but reservedly—to your boss. Watson must keep her objective in mind: to make Holt understand why her performance may be uneven, so that he preserves his regard for her. Without being dramatic or inflamatory, she should tell Holt only what he needs to know: "My husband and I are going through a divorce which is becoming messy, and I want to apologize now if I've seemed distracted lately."

By sparing him the gory details, she prevents herself from seeming a victim or martyr like Howe. Watson needs to underscore her professionalism and reassure her boss of her commitment to work by promising to make up for any lapses.

As for co-workers, she should let them know about the divorce, but be tight-lipped about details with all but her most trusted friends. During lunch or after a distressing phone call, she might mention that she is in the middle of a divorce but resist the temptation to play her colleagues for sympathy as Howe does.

As many social psychologists have noted, men, in general, feel more comfortable in impersonal work environments, while women tend to thrive on emotional connections. As a result, women often find it easier to talk to female bosses than to male bosses. And those who work in male-dominated companies find that employees who are more open than the unspoken rules of the workplace allow are often seen as less reliable.

With more women entering the ranks of upper management, such institutional taboos are losing their potency. Even so, those employees who suffer from chronic problems—a long-standing illness or a drawn-out divorce—need to be careful about seeking too much sympathy; eventually, even the most tolerant and understanding may lose patience with them.

And, of course, bigotry and ignorance exist in all kinds of

offices. Weigh the possible reactions to potentially controversial disclosures before determining how much to reveal. If your boss is a homophobe, then it might be wise to tell him that your brother-in-law is dying without mentioning that he is gay and has AIDS. Similarly, if you think your reputation would suffer if you disclosed that your husband is filing for bankruptcy or is in a drug rehabilitation program, then tell only as much of the truth as you think your company needs to know.

Fair or not, your colleagues are not your friends. Your only obligation is to keep them informed about issues related to your work. Tell them just enough to help them understand the situation so that you can preserve your reputation.

PART FOUR

TRIGGERING
YOUR
AMBITION

he alphabetical placement of ambition puts it somewhere between ambiguity and ambivalence—not unlike its role in our lives. Ambition is our right to admit to our yearning to participate, achieve, and succeed. And it requires a plan, even though it's a plan we probably won't follow completely. Unfortunately, if we don't have a plan, we will fall victim to the plans of others. If we're smart, we have to learn to adjust, modify, and change our plan according to the marketplace or the opportunities that we encounter. If we don't, then we live totally with the consequences of fate.

Finding what we want—even when we don't really know what it is from the outset—is one of the central missions of our lives. Many of us gravitate toward what we want, "connecting the dots" of our interests along the way. Others fall into something we come to discover is "home," and enjoy honing our skills in a comfortable situation. Others continue to search. Yet no matter where we are in our career, we still have to fan our own fires of inspiration and ambition, the creativity that is contagious in mobilizing and motivating others as well.

In this final section, we'll concentrate on making ambition an integral part of our work lives.

SHOULD YOU PUSH HARD FOR A PROMOTION?

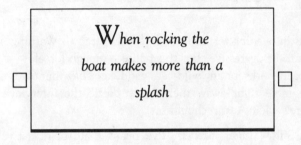

When rocking the
boat makes more than a
splash

When Barbara Austin returns from her business lunch, she's elated. A colleague has just tipped her off to an opening in consumer-products lending, the high-power department of the Chicago commercial bank where she's a vice president. What a coup it would be if she could snag the position. She'd make much more money, boost her prestige, and launch her career.

In the five years since she graduated from business school, Austin has worked in the bank's credit department, reviewing and analyzing corporate loans. It's interesting work, but recently Austin has been itching to move on. Now's her opportunity.

There are several hitches, however. Austin is afraid that her somewhat territorial supervisor, Kathryn Herman, will find out she's looking for another job. Austin also knows she'll be competing with people who have a lot more marketing experience, not to mention direct client contact, which she's never had. So she's not sure how to present herself to Tom Washington, the senior VP who heads consumer-products lending. Can she go around company policy, which dictates that internal moves be initiated through personnel? How aggressively should she go after this opportunity?

☐   # A GAME PLAN FOR A WILD-CARD CANDIDATE   ☐

Austin is going for a sales job, so her pitch to Washington has to be aggressive. But this polite—though forceful—approach works for any wild-card candidate. Lay your cards on the table right away, then try to dazzle the interviewer. Here's what Austin should say:

AUSTIN *(after niceties):* I've heard that you're actively looking for a consumer-products lender. Is that right?

WASHINGTON: Right you are. I've been swamped with résumés and calls.

AUSTIN: Great. I think I can help you out. Let me tell you why I'm right for the job: First, you have all these investment people out of work. They're desperate to find a job—any job—to tide them over. That's not where I'm coming from. I had the luxury of waiting for the right opening to come along—and this is it.

What I bring are first-rate analytical skills. I can tell clients what they need and why they need it. I've come to learn all the ins and outs of loans and credit in my research. I track my loan recommendations, and it drives me crazy when I see some clients ask for loans that are too low or the wrong kind.

WASHINGTON: I've heard you do great work, but this is a marketing job. What makes you think you can handle it?

AUSTIN: I'm not shy, and I'm not afraid to be aggressive.

With my research background, I can bring real information to the clients, I can answer their questions, and I can guide them in structuring their transactions. From what I've heard about you, that's the kind of responsible lending you're after. True?

WASHINGTON: Absolutely. I wish I could take the chance—you certainly show initiative. But, truthfully, you don't have the track record for it.

AUSTIN: I understand your concerns, so let me offer you a risk-free proposition: Give me the job for six months and let me prove myself. I'll work harder than anyone you've ever seen. I'm sure you'll be pleased, but if you're not I'll go back to research without a fuss. I'm that willing to bet on my skills.

What works in Austin's pitch? She anticipated Washington's objections and turned her liabilities into assets. And she did her homework. She found out, for instance, that Washington valued substantive, loyal employees, and she played on that knowledge. When the heat was on, she threw in a preplanned trump card, the fact that she would be willing to be put on probation. By playing it smart, Austin can be assured that even if it doesn't work out this time, Washington will remember her.

☐ ☐

STRATEGY

BEFORE Austin navigates these tricky waters, she should decide whether rocking the boat is really worth it. Her first move is to do some investigating to find out what the job is like—and whether she'll do well in it.

Austin doesn't have the luxury of using the interview to

gather information. So she should tap into the corporate grapevine to find out why the opening exists, what the rate of employee turnover is, whether any women have ever been hired in that area, and what their tenures have been. In the process, Austin will be able to discover what it's like to work in consumer-products lending, where the department's energies are being directed, and what qualities Washington might be looking for in his staff. She also should try to get the scoop on Washington's management style and personality.

Facts in hand, Austin will be in a better position to take step two: making a clear evaluation of her internal motivations and skills, and deciding whether they jibe with the realities of the position.

In this case, Austin needs to ask herself whether she has the ability—and interest—to move successfully from the technical side of research and analysis to the transactional side, closing the deal. Has she ever initiated a program, made a presentation, or sold a product or service? Was she on the debate team in school? Does she enjoy the negotiation process (buying or selling a house, say, or bargaining for merchandise)? Does she get excited thinking about these things? Does she avoid any of them? Does she prefer knowing everything about a subject, or closing the deal?

Austin must be willing to risk failing or being fired if her plan backfires or if commercial lending doesn't turn out to be her thing. It's a risky proposition, but taking smart risks is part of hitting in the big leagues, of rising in an organization, and gaining responsibility and rewards in the tighter team play among top managers.

If Austin decides the risk is worth it, she needs to be aggressive in order to land the job. That means bypassing the lower-level corporate protocol of going through personnel or other formal channels, and dealing directly with the source, the senior VP who's doing the hiring.

Moving up is about being a player, making direct connections—not signing up and standing in line like a good student. It's a myth that in the business world if you're good you'll be discovered. Waiting to be chosen only paralyzes you. Being *proactive* has to become an automatic impulse.

Another factor Austin needs to consider before she talks to anyone: corporate gossip. If she goes after the job, chances are her boss soon will find out, and the news will come as a particularly unwelcome surprise if it's heard from a third party. Therefore Austin must deal with her boss first. If they work well together, then she'd be crazy not to involve Herman, especially if her boss has any kind of rapport with Washington.

Austin has to tell Herman that she's confiding in her because she admires her and that she wants more than her advice—she wants her blessing. She has to cast Herman not as an abandoned boss but as a confidante/mentor. Is this manipulation? You bet—of the best kind. Austin is recognizing the strength of Herman's position and speaking to it; she is taking her future into her own hands.

Will it work? Maybe. But at least Austin has laid the groundwork and is ready for her biggest job yet: convincing Washington that she's able to handle the heavy marketing and client contact intrinsic to consumer-products lending even though she lacks the appropriate experience.

Austin now has the perfect opportunity to prove her sales abilities by selling herself to Washington. She should address her marketing inexperience head-on rather than hope he won't notice because he's impressed by her other skills. And she should talk to him in person, not hide behind the overestimated strategy of sending him her résumé. People often think that's an aggressive act in itself, when in fact it's passive and puts all of the responsibility—and power—in the hands of the hirer.

Austin should call Washington directly to set up a meeting. Once there, she has to show him not only that she has an excellent track record but that she'll be an asset to his department in this vulnerable financial market. She has to make him see her as a different but equally competent salesperson: one who has the background to fortify her pitch with an in-depth understanding of the market and of the client companies' needs.

Doing all this prep work is going to take time out of Austin's already tight schedule. There may not be a payoff. But Austin has taken the risk of investing in herself. A move that, ultimately, will make her a success.

BURNED OUT:
CAN YOU GET FIRED
UP AGAIN?

> **W**hen you've completed
> the three stages of a job cycle,
> you burn out—and it's time
> to leap to new terrain.

Lately Susan O'Brien has been finding it harder and harder to get up for work. She feels bored and depleted of energy. Small triumphs that would have thrilled her a year ago don't do much to motivate her now. O'Brien, the director of human resources for a large national bank, has earned considerable recognition for her successes from both the bank and her professional associates. Her boss, senior vice president Tony Breddo, though more conservative by nature than she, nonetheless admires her work and offers her unsolicited praise. Moreover, O'Brien is vested in the bank. She's as financially secure as anyone she knows. And yet . . .

O'Brien started in human resources at a competing bank sixteen years ago, after graduating from a small liberal arts college. She was promoted quickly, having spent three arduous years taking night classes for her MBA. Seven years ago she joined the bank where she now works. In her four-year tenure as director of human resources, overseeing twenty-eight people, O'Brien has developed a reputation as a gifted manager.

She has restructured the department, rewritten the bank's health-care policy, introduced new, parent-friendly benefits, and honed the employees' retirement investment plan. She's published journal articles and has given speeches at industry conferences. Last year she was president of the local chapter of her professional association. She likes being a leader and is pleased that others appreciate her efforts. But while she's taken pleasure in organizing and managing others, as well as being their advocate, she just doesn't enjoy her work anymore.

O'Brien can't explain her malaise. She doesn't know what she wants to do next, much less how to go about doing it. A few weeks ago, a colleague who was director of personnel at a competing bank left to join a booming management-consulting group and invited O'Brien to join, too. But that has only the momentary appeal of change for its own sake. The fact is, she enjoys the banking world and knows she belongs in a corporate structure. It's just that there's nothing left in human resources that she looks forward to exploring. O'Brien is unwilling to begin at the bottom again in another area. And even if she could handle that, what is it she'd do?

HOW TO FIND YOUR NEXT NICHE

For several weeks now, O'Brien has been trying to find topics that spark her interest. The closest she's come is a newspaper article about an employee trend. It's just the seed of an idea, but that's enough for now. She could continue her exploration by bringing up the article in an informal brainstorming session with her boss, Tony Breddo, the person who has the power to turn her idea into an opportunity.

O'BRIEN: Did you see this article in the *Times* about part-time executives?

BREDDO: Yeah, interesting.

O'BRIEN *(laughing):* I guess we're cutting edge, because we've been hiring more part-timers and consultants for a while.

BREDDO: Saves us money in benefits.

O'BRIEN: I bet we could do better than that. Has anyone experimented with selling benefits to part-timers at lower rates?

BREDDO: Other than professional groups? I don't think so . . . but it's not a bad idea.

O'BRIEN: The economic climate has changed so dramatically in the past few years—and not just in human resources. There are whole new markets that never existed before for commercial banks—pensions, college funds, mortgages . . .

BREDDO: It's odd you're bringing this up right now. I just had a similar conversation with Learner over in PR.

O'BRIEN: Maybe there's something to this. How about if we get a group of people together from different departments to share their insights on the future of the new markets?

BREDDO: We could use some sort of task force, but I don't have time to organize anything like that right now.

O'BRIEN: Leave it to me. I'll coordinate the whole thing, and find a way to communicate what we find.

What worked in O'Brien's approach? She subtly brought up a past accomplishment—hiring part-timers— and threw out her new idea in a nonthreatening way. She also listened to Breddo and took each of his responses one step further, reminding him that she's good to brainstorm with. O'Brien's clincher: asking for what she wants and getting Breddo's backing. She made it clear that she expects to chair the task force and thus assures herself a role as a leader in the new arena.

☐   ☐

STRATEGY

O'BRIEN has all the earmarks of burnout. She's completed the "learn-do-teach" cycle of work. Once it is completed, achievers move on to begin another cycle: learning something new—either another aspect of the same job or something altogether fresh. When you make the mistake of remaining in one of the cycle's phases too long, spinning your wheels, you suffer. That's burnout.

The symptoms of burnout are just like those of depression: At first there's discouragement, a sense that you're incapable of regaining motivation for work. Then, if you don't take action, this hopelessness seeps into all areas of your life. If you still do nothing, you begin to feel helpless, unable to change the situation. Finally you withdraw.

Having just passed through a successful phase as a top-level manager, O'Brien is clearly trapped at the end of the "teach" phase of her career cycle. Now's the time for her to take a big leap to unknown terrain. But hearing that message—even wanting to respond—is easier than commanding herself to act. Taking action is especially difficult because O'Brien doesn't have any idea what the nature of her next cycle should be.

How can O'Brien motivate herself to take that step? The way all achievers do—by connecting herself to some new ideas and finding one that takes root. It's not a blind gamble, but it is risky. It has been a long time since O'Brien made a foray into unknown territory. Suppose she looks ignorant or feels stupid, not at all like the competent director she has been. Beneath the surface lies the very real fear that she will lose her reputation, her identity, even her career.

Should O'Brien take the chance? Like the message in a Chinese fortune cookie, the answer lies tightly wrapped in her psyche, which has begun to shrivel from lack of stimulation. O'Brien *has* to look for more stimulating professional outlets.

What O'Brien should not do is react by quitting and looking around for something better. To change jobs without serious investigation and preparation is unlikely to bring her success. She'll only carry her depression with her. Instead O'Brien should take on a new challenge while continuing in her present job. She has little risk of losing it, as she can get through the day-to-day work with minimal effort.

Over the next few weeks, O'Brien should take advantage of her position and start making lunch and dinner dates with those colleagues whose professional opinions she admires. The point of these get-togethers is to informally brainstorm. Without giving any hint of her burnout, she should begin a dialogue about the bank's future, asking her co-workers to share their thoughts on likely projects. Perhaps something they say will excite her or, at the very least, get her thinking.

Instead of reading more about human resources, she should try to discover new topics. Her goal is to find a project that is commercially sound and advantageous for the bank. When O'Brien finds something even close to what she wants to work on, she should try to carve out a niche for herself as an expert in that particular field. Then she can solicit her boss's support and maneuver her transition to another division of the bank.

I once had a client who was frustrated in her job as head of personnel at an international restaurant corporation. I suggested instead of complaining about her boredom to her boss—which would only annoy him—that she ask him where he wanted the company to go in the next five years and how she could help him take it there. Among other things, he spoke of opening up new territories in foreign countries. Catching her interest, he challenged her to create a task force to start the wheels in motion. Within six months she had replaced herself as director of personnel—and was heading the new overseas operation.

Taking such risks of exploration is part of the process of uncovering an unknown or obscure vocation. O'Brien needs to love herself enough to physically leave what she has already left emotionally—and move on. Learning, conceptualizing, changing, and growing are what's missing in her life. Most people need to change arenas at some point in their careers. The ones who succeed create opportunities out of that transition.

YOUR FANTASY CAREER: SHOULD YOU GO FOR IT?

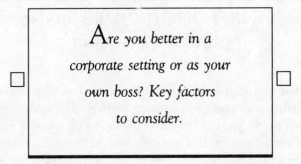

Are you better in a corporate setting or as your own boss? Key factors to consider.

Michelle Gordon, a sales manager at a national architectural firm, has watched her company trim its ranks as it struggles to survive in an industry beset by hard times. But instead of feeling saddened by the cutbacks and worrying about her own job security, Gordon finds herself fantasizing about being laid off and starting her own business. Though she doesn't seem to be in danger of losing her position, for the past few years Gordon has felt underused and frustrated by the bureaucracy at her firm. She has a secret dream of opening a gallery for the decorative arts—her lifelong passion.

Gordon holds two degrees in art history and has an impressive collection of Navajo rugs and pots. For the past three years she has worked as a volunteer for the city's annual arts festival, serving first as an assistant, then as co-chair, and this year as chairwoman. Under her leadership, this year's festival was the largest and most successful yet in the number of dollars raised.

Gordon knows that she has a great eye and good common sense, and that she is adept at handling difficult and demanding clients—and she is a super saleswoman. Her job is to convince builders, developers, and bankers to use her firm's services. But she has never run a business. Could she function on her own, without the protection and security of a large firm? Before she takes the risk of quitting her job, she needs to find out.

☐ NINE TOUGH QUESTIONS ☐
TO ASK YOURSELF

Before you start your own business, you should determine whether you have the necessary psychological makeup; in other words, you need to have a dialogue with yourself. Here are some questions that will help you get it started. Answer each with a number from one to ten, with 1 being "never" and 10 being "always."

- Have I managed projects without supervision?
- Do I initiate projects and carry them through successfully?
- Have I enjoyed being in charge?
- Can I hire and fire others when necessary?
- Can I delegate work?
- Do I criticize others' work when necessary—and get what I need?
- Can I negotiate and compromise without feeling like I'm selling out?
- Do I have abundant energy?
- Can I delay gratification—put off buying luxuries, and even some basic necessities—to attain a goal?

If you consistently rated yourself lower than five, come out of hiding: whether you stay in the corporate world or try to go out on your own, your aversion to risk will hold you back. If you scored fives, sixes, sevens, and eights, increase your level of risk so that you become adept at taking chances. If your scores were nines or tens, you may be ready to go out on your own. It could also mean that you are ready to rise into upper management. Only you can decide.

☐   ☐

STRATEGY

RUNNING one's own business is a common fantasy. Women and men were recently polled separately about their top five dream jobs, and owning a business was the only occupation that was on both lists.

It's not surprising. The idea of ownership taps into wishes for freedom—freedom from bosses, restrictive policies, and anything else that might rob you of credit and creativity.

For women, the dream is also fueled by frustrations with the glass ceiling, that invisible barrier beyond which women cannot advance in the corporate world. As more of us have bumped against it, the number of female entrepreneurs has risen dramatically. Nearly one-third of all entrepreneurs surveyed by the Internal Revenue Service in 1987 were female; by the year 2000, it is estimated, women will own half of all businesses in the country.

As powerful as the underlying motivation may be, however, it is not enough to make a business succeed. One study by the Small Business Administration (SBA) found that roughly one out of four new businesses dissolves within two years. The most obvious reason for business failure is insufficient capital. Gordon, of course, needs to do the necessary market research and business planning before she tries to open a gallery. There are many excellent books and organizations she can turn to for guidance.

Equally important—and more often overlooked—is the psychological dimension of launching a business. Some people are just better suited to the corporate world than to entrepreneurship. They like its security and stability, and being in the corporate world enables them to turn their private dreams into much grander projects than they could realize on their own.

One point about that list of dream jobs: All of them were on the fantasy end of the spectrum. ("Forest ranger" turned up frequently on the men's lists—how many men would want the reality?) What that suggests is that for many people launching a business is just a daydream, not something they should act upon. It may be a reaction to a too-tough boss or to feeling bored and unchallenged by their work. Some people may retreat into the fantasy of having their own business instead of trying to create a situation in the corporate environment that would fulfill their needs.

Should Gordon strike out on her own? Just as she needs to research the nuts and bolts of her business, she needs to examine her hopes and desires. This assessment process can take place over a period of months. Here are some of the major points Gordon should consider.

☐ *The reality principle.* Sometimes what attracts a person to a business is at odds with reality. For example, I once had a client who left a large corporation to become a consultant. He was bored and unchallenged, and thought consulting would be more exciting. But he neglected to consider that he enjoyed the power of being a boss whom others would follow unquestioningly. As a consultant, you have to make suggestions, not commands. Not surprisingly, his consulting business was a failure.

Gordon also needs to be realistic. Running a decorative-arts gallery won't be like decorating her house; she won't be collecting for her own pleasure. To sell in volume she will have to figure out what the public wants. Since she has already learned to put aside her own tastes in architecture as a saleswoman, there is good reason to believe that she could make the adjustment.

☐   *The solo factor.* In a corporation, you go through channels, sit on committees, and consult with your superiors. Some people don't mind that. They may even appreciate the input of others and the fact that they aren't entirely responsible for a decision. But they probably should not become entrepreneurs.

Entrepreneurs need to be decisive and able to handle the pressure of knowing it's all on your shoulders. Until you put yourself in such a situation, it will be difficult for you to know whether you have this ability.

Gordon demonstrated a willingness to assume this burden when she ran the arts festival. Because the festival was understaffed, she often made snap decisions. She thought of herself as "winging it." The truth is that she relished the freedom from her firm's bureaucracy and could handle the risk of being wrong.

Typically, successful entrepreneurs will tell you that they appreciate the freedom to make their own decisions, unconstrained by someone else's rules and policies. They want people to belong to *their* organization and follow *their* rules.

☐   *Risk tolerance.* Owning a business is fraught with risk. Every day your ability to respond will be challenged. If business is slow, you have to be able to think of innovative ways to bring in more customers. If a contractor demands more money to finish a project that you need finished immediately, you have to figure out a solution—fast. Handling risk is so critical that I don't recommend that anyone launch a business without having demonstrated a high tolerance for it.

Gordon hasn't taken professional risks, but she took a personal one by having her name associated with the arts festival. If the festival had failed, it would have been her disaster.

What she needs to figure out is whether now is the right time for her to take this particular risk. That can be assessed only with a business plan and market research.

☐   *Creating a network.* In a corporation, you won't rise far without a network. But as an entrepreneur, your very survival depends on it. In a recent survey by the Center for Advanced Purchasing Studies in Tempe, Arizona, women vendors cited old-boy networks as a major reason why they didn't win corporate contracts. Business is done by networking, and those who aren't plugged in get left out.

Gordon needs a network of experts whom she has called on before and feels comfortable calling on again. Like risk taking, using networks requires practice.

Fortunately Gordon already has a strong network through her art collecting and her work at the arts festival. And as a saleswoman, she has become comfortable with using contacts to seal deals.

☐   *The dream of all dreams.* This can't be just another one of your great ideas. It should be a calling. You should feel that if you don't try out this business venture, you will have failed yourself. Without that passion and commitment, you will not make it through the tough times—and, invariably, there *are* tough times.

Launching a business involves great sacrifices of time and money. A computer consultant I know left a cushy job at IBM to start her own training company. Her diet consisted largely of peanut-butter sandwiches just so she could cover her office rent. To her the sacrifice was worth it because she was creating what she wanted to, and the creation was all hers. It took her a full year before she turned a profit and could even dine out.

In corroboration, the SBA says the average business takes ten months to two years before it turns a profit. In the meantime, every aspect of the business—accounting, sales, operations, even cleaning—is your responsibility, around the clock. The corporate world is set up as a hierarchy in which you are responsible for only one part of the picture. But in your business, you play all roles.

Gordon has to be willing to devote her attention not only

to filling the gallery with interesting artworks but also to devising an appropriate billing system and installing phone lines. Having run the arts festival on a shoestring budget—all staffers answered their own phones and did their own photocopying—she already has demonstrated that she can handle such challenges. And she has been interested in the decorative arts since she was an art history student twenty years ago. Owning the gallery would be connecting the dots of her lifelong interest.

But what if you find that you aren't psychologically suited to being an entrepreneur? It only means that you will need to inject the creativity, passion, and freshness you crave into the company you work for. The company won't do that for you, but you can take on a new project, starting a partnership with another office, or even taking on pro bono work. What counts is that you continue to challenge yourself and continue to grow—whether it's inside or outside the corporate world.

FIRED:
CAN YOU LEARN
FROM IT?

*A pink slip can be
a ticket to nowhere—or to the
executive suite. This decision
is in your hands.*

Jennifer Ritt is on edge. Three weeks ago she lost her job in a major pharmaceutical company's product group. Her boss, Jim Hanley, told her that his two product groups were being merged to increase efficiency and that some jobs had to be cut. Hers was one of them. He was careful to use all the euphemisms—"let go," "pink-slipped," "downsizing"—but the bottom line was that Ritt was unemployed.

Friends tried to console her, telling her that she was just a victim of the bad economy. In fact, 10 percent of the staff—nine people, including herself—had lost their jobs. All were given relatively generous severance packages. Ritt tried to be positive; she reminded herself that she could now take that vacation to the Orient that she had always dreamed about. But she couldn't shake the awful suspicion that she had somehow failed and that this "layoff" was actually a firing.

Hanley and Ritt had never clicked. He used to make fun of

her rapid-fire way of talking, moving his fingers together as if they were chattering teeth. And seven months ago he gave her a lukewarm appraisal, suggesting that she needed to show more initiative. She had attempted to heed his warning, but the truth was that she felt his criticism was unfair. After all, she always did all of her work. What more did Hanley want?

Ritt wants to believe that her friends are right, that she was just a victim of circumstance. But she wonders: Might she have been one of the ones kept on had she performed differently? Or is she just being paranoid?

☐ THE EARLY-WARNING TEST ☐

You're unhappy at work? Take this quiz to find out whether it's because the company is in trouble or because you are the real source of the problem.

1. *My company is . . .*
   A. Too bureaucratic
   B. Coping well
   C. Unresponsive to me

2. *My boss is . . .*
   A. Over the hill
   B. Great
   C. A political operator

3. *My co-workers are . . .*
   A. Worried
   B. Underworked
   C. Too cliquish

4. *In my company I'm known as . . .*
   A. A hard worker
   B. An ace pinch hitter
   C. A devil's advocate

5. *Time spent wishing I were elsewhere:*
   A. 30%
   B. 20%
   C. 65%

6. *When I wake up, I feel . . .*
   A. Nervous
   B. Eager
   C. Depressed

If you've checked off mostly A's, you've picked up cues that your company is hurting. Start networking. Don't be caught short. If you chose more B's, then you are valued by your company and have a reasonably secure job. Appreciate it. If you responded mostly with C's, then you need to make changes within yourself. You are probably unhappy with your job because you're suffering from poor self-esteem. Consider taking dance lessons or a public-speaking class, or engaging in another activity that will build confidence and social grace. Only then will you be able to take action on the job. Bad economic times call for innovation, especially your own.

□   □

STRATEGY

WHEN you lose a job, it's normal, and quite healthy, to go through a grieving period. Part of what makes getting fired so traumatic is that it shatters the illusion that your job—and your place in the world—is guaranteed.

But that's an illusion best shattered. No job is totally secure. These days even IBM lays off people. According to a study by the New York-based outplacement firm Drake Beam Morin, Inc., only about 6 percent of 1,200 unemployed executives surveyed were terminated because of the quality of their work. The majority were casualties of retrenchment. The hard times that began with the nineties promise to continue, so chances are no matter how savvy, bright, or talented you are, you may find yourself out of a job.

The key, then, is to learn from the experience and move on. To accomplish this, you first need to accept the loss and then take a hard look at what happened: What, if anything, could you have done to prevent your being fired?

In Ritt's case, there was a clear indication seven months before she was laid off that Hanley wasn't satisfied with her performance. He told her that she wasn't showing enough initiative. Hanley wasn't firing her; he was giving her a second chance. What Ritt should have done then was to find out exactly what Hanley wanted from her and her work. If she had asked him that, she might have understood why he didn't see her as a go-getter. Then she might have been able to take the steps necessary to show Hanley that she took his word seriously and wanted his approval. Later she could have asked him, "How am I doing, boss?" And she might have heard an answer she liked.

Instead, Ritt appeared to not do much of anything. That made it seem like she was deliberately ignoring her boss's advice (which was really a command). So when push came to shove and Hanley's two departments merged, Ritt was viewed as one of the expendables.

In good times slow runners may be tolerated. But the reality is that during hard times, when employers have to eliminate staff, they often take the opportunity to weed out those people who are unproductive, relatively unpopular, or somehow ill suited to their jobs. And these employees usually know who they are. They're generally unhappy at their jobs but stay because they either don't have the courage to quit or are just lazy.

Ritt needs to ask herself why she didn't follow Hanley's suggestions. Perhaps she was bored and unconsciously desired a change in her job, perhaps even in her career. If so, now is the time—and the opportunity—to figure out what she really would like to be doing. Yet the first thing people do when they lose a job is try to find another job just like it. The smarter approach is to explore alternatives and hidden interests.

But how can she prevent herself from getting into this situation again? In her next job Ritt should do everything she can to get management to view her as indispensable. That means doing more than the job's basic requirements. She must work at making her boss, co-workers, and clients dependent on her. Ritt should have been creating proposals to salvage business at her former company, since her division was in trouble, and supporting Hanley. If I could have interviewed those who were kept on at Ritt's company, I am sure I would have found that most have close working relationships with their supervisors.

And yet, being indispensable isn't an insurance policy against losing your job. You may be an extraordinarily intelligent and highly competent employee with the misfortune of having a politically weak or unsophisticated boss, one who can't (or won't) fight to save your job. Or maybe you're working on a money-losing account, product, or project that the company wants to eliminate. Sometimes being laid off amounts to random firing, and the situation is truly out of your control. In these cases you need to give yourself a break and remind yourself that it wasn't your fault.

But that's not all you should do. There's something to be learned no matter what the particulars. You should always try to have a broad perspective. Look at the big picture, and look ahead. Keeping your job isn't just about doing your work well. If you have a weak boss, try to make yourself known to some of the key players in the company. If you are working in a losing division or a shrinking field, think about transferring or moving into a new field so you don't go down with the ship.

Of course, it may be that none of this will prevent your being laid off. But keep this in mind: Without exception, everyone I've ever known who has been fired has gone on to have a more fulfilling, successful career because he or she has learned from the experience. Not a bad trade, if you are strong enough.

WANT TO QUIT?
WHY YOU SHOULDN'T

> **I**f you're bored
> and frustrated, take your
> job and re-create it.

In her ten years in the real estate division of a major bank, Diana Searles has never seen a market as dead as this one. While she used to spend her days juggling deals, she now struggles to fill her time by reading newspapers, attending conferences, taking long lunches, and working out at the gym.

While it's been a sociable time, even a relaxing one, the tedium is beginning to frustrate Searles. Once easygoing and good-natured, she has become a short-tempered complainer. What she wants—what she is aching for—is a promotion. Even before the market collapsed, she was starting to feel the itch. Then it seemed possible that she would be promoted in the near future. Now it's hopeless. Her bank has been downsizing, and half of her department has been laid off in the past six months. Those with jobs—including her supervisor—are staying put.

Her friends tell her that she should just be happy she has a job. But she isn't. The absence of work has been driving her crazy with boredom, so crazy that she has even contemplated jeopardizing her mortgage by quitting and finding a new job. And then, at a luncheon last week, Searles found herself sitting next to a friend's friend, an executive recruiter. They exchanged cards, and now, back at her office, Searles wonders whether she should make that critical call. It could take a year to find another job; the process would be time-consuming and exhausting. Maybe her friends are right—perhaps she should just try to endure the boredom until the economy improves. But how long will that be?

☐ # SHOULD YOU ☐
STAY OR LEAVE?
A QUIZ

Most people have difficulty identifying whether they need to quit or reinvigorate the job they have. But there are signs. Answer the following questions to find out what your next step should be.

- Has your boss been avoiding you or excluding you from meetings?
- Is there a new supervisor who seems to have been hired as a "hatchet man," eliminating jobs—possibly yours?
- Has your mentor seemed depressed, perhaps over the knowledge that more jobs will go, maybe even yours?
- Do your professional contacts reveal that your company is heading for a worse turn?
- Have you been rebuffed the last four times you have suggested a new plan or requested joining a successful project?
- Is the one department that seems to be picking up speed headed by someone who dislikes you?

If you answered yes to some or all of these questions, consider leaving. You have no doubt known this for a long time but have been actively denying the ugly truth. (If your only *yes* was to the fifth question, then you need to focus on learning how to motivate and persuade others, fortunately, a lot easier to accomplish than finding a new job.) If you answered *no* to most questions, then your dilemma lies within you; you need to reinvent the job you have and transform it into the job you want. Use the following questions to begin that process:

- If the economy were to pick up today, what would be the first project you would undertake? Can you start it now so that you may create a market, or at least be prepared when the economy does change?
- If you had another title, what would that allow you to do that you're not doing now? How can you perform those duties now anyway?
- If you were to create an intellectual salon at work, whom would you invite and what would you discuss? Can you hold an exploratory meeting of such a group this week?

☐   ☐

STRATEGY

IN today's economy many of us share with Searles that schizophrenic reaction to a saved job: relieved to be spared, yet frustrated by the failure of the company to sustain the former level of business. Always lurking in the back of our mind is the fantasy of quitting and starting over. While this is unquestionably an option to consider, it should not be the first attempt at a solution.

The reality is that in a tight economy there are fewer promotions and fewer new positions. You diminish your chance of snagging one of those rare opportunities when you are depressed. A job search at such a time is never the ideal tactic, for you will take your shadow with you—the feeling of being out of control and the insecurity about your skills. If you do get a new position, it will most likely be a lateral move.

But there is another reason why a job hunt isn't the answer to Searles's predicament: demographics. The numbers are against the baby boomers. There are so many of them that at some point everyone will plateau; people will not be able to rise at the same rapid rate as they did in the eighties. Chances are, no matter what industry you're in, you will find yourself stuck and unable to get a promotion. Even when this recession passes, promotions will be harder and harder to come by for baby boomers. Leaping to a new company will not change that fact.

Before Searles starts searching for another job, she should try to use the current downtime at the bank. She might, for instance, learn about topics that will be valuable when her industry revives. She might consider studying for an advanced license or degree in urban planning, architecture, or finance. Or she might use the time to improve her profile by getting involved in the politics of real estate and serving on city or state committees. She could also start a task force within her company to study a long-standing problem plaguing the bank. At the least, she will improve her spirits by getting involved and focusing again on her career. At best, she will learn how to catapult herself out of her malaise and forge new business skills. She might even create a new project that proves to be critical to the well-being of her company.

Most achievers I've known have sought challenges rather than wait for others to assign tasks to them. For example, some real estate experts have broadened their careers by creating new departments in universities or investing in new retail projects. Having outside ventures while maintaining their jobs satisfied their need for security as well as their desire for adventure. Others have gradually shifted their responsibilities by acquiring new ones while maintaining their old ones. A loan officer at a huge national bank now manages its large and well-regarded art collection; another branch manager is the governmental-relations liaison, handling all of the bank's dealings with state and federal officials.

If Searles were to analyze the real estate market and financial services, she might also recognize untapped opportunities for herself in the field. When you think of it, most innovations and new solutions come during troubled times. In healthy times, few are inspired to create improved products or services or work beyond what is required; perspective is usually shortsighted. Hard economic times require you to take action and use foresight.

Instead of wasting time in aimless chitchat, Searles should brainstorm with real estate experts—developers, urban planners, architects, brokers, bankers, sociologists, and futurists. Together they could come up with inventive solutions to tough problems. Take the explosion of single mothers, for example. A company could serve them by building a development in which women could live together in large group homes or newly built apartments with central function rooms and quarters for retirees who might run the "household." Such an innovative response to a desperate need could reinvigorate her bank—and her job.

Searles would also do herself a great favor if she gave up on her immature insistence that her industry be perfect in order for her to be engaged with it and interested in her job. She should recognize the fact that all industries operate in cycles. She is behaving as if the eighties boom was the norm, as if it should have continued indefinitely, when the boom was just one part of the cycle.

In one regard, her friends are right—she should stop complaining. No matter how justified her gripes, complaining serves only to undermine what little morale is left in the department and shut down any vision of more positive alternatives. It even brands her as churlish and childish. Once Searles accepts the roller-coaster nature of business and adjusts her work habits to it, she will find herself able to thrive—in all economic conditions.

AVOIDING THE
MOMMY-TRACK TRAP

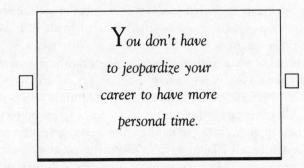

You don't have
to jeopardize your
career to have more
personal time.

Ann Winograd is living out her fantasy of having it all. A highly regarded advertising executive, she is happily married to a successful radiologist, and they have a two-year-old daughter. There's only one problem: Winograd is on the verge of collapse. She just can't continue to put in those grinding fourteen-hour days.

She starts at five-thirty with an exercise session, followed by a fast breakfast with her husband and daughter and then instructions to the baby-sitter—all before she arrives at the office at six forty-five. Once she is at work, Winograd's day is packed with interesting but high-pressure meetings in which she must make decisions, resolve disputes between her agency and clients, and motivate her creative but temperamental staff. Between meetings, she manages to make a few calls to her baby-sitter.

At six-thirty she leaves the office, stopping on her way home to pick up a few items for dinner. By the time she has finished eating at eight, Winograd is exhausted.

Winograd and her husband have recently begun talking about having a second child. But there isn't any room in her schedule for downtime now; lately even weekends have been taken up with emergency work sessions at home or, worse, in the office. How can she possibly consider having another baby?

Winograd's closest friend, Pat Fields, a partner in a prestigious law firm, has been advising her to do what she does: work part-time. But Fields admits that her colleagues seem to have less respect for her now, and some clearly view her as a "mommy-tracker," a woman who is less serious about her career than fast-trackers are. Winograd secretly wonders whether they aren't right. Work has become less central to Fields's identity; now it's just a way to pay her bills. Winograd doesn't want to give up her full-out commitment to her career. Yet she knows she can't continue to meet the growing demands of both her firm and her family. Can she change any part of her work life without becoming a mommy-tracker?

□ · SHORTEN YOUR DAY □
(BUT NOT YOUR PAY)

Winograd wants to continue to work full-time, but not on a twelve-hour-a-day schedule. By stressing that she will produce the same results without all the overtime, she convinces her boss, Tom Emerson, executive vice president of the firm, to let her try a thirty-five to forty-hour week. Just after a client meeting that went particularly well, she steps into his office.

WINOGRAD: Tom, I'd like to propose a new work schedule—one that will make me more efficient than I have been.

EMERSON: So far, it sounds good.

WINOGRAD: As you know, I've been routinely working

twelve-hour days. I am sure that I can accomplish my work in seven or eight hours a day. What I'd like to do is cut back to a thirty-five to forty-hour week. I would still be as productive as I have been, except I would do it within a nine-to-five day. How does that sound?

EMERSON: You know the firm is going through some rough times. I need to be able to count on you to be here when I need you.

WINOGRAD: Of course I'll be available if an emergency arises, but I am confident that I can be equally productive without working the hours I've been keeping. I would schedule all meetings from nine to five instead of at seven p.m. or eight a.m.

If I don't change my pace, I'll burn out. I know that you haven't been able to tell the stress I've been under because I've been trying to hide it. At this point, I never have time for a relaxed meal at home with my family.

EMERSON: I understand that you want to spend more time with your baby. Have you thought about hiring a live-in housekeeper? That made my sister's life a lot easier.

WINOGRAD: We already have a baby-sitter, and I thought that would solve our problems, too. But what I found out was that no one could replace me when it came to eating dinner with my family.

EMERSON: I hear what you're saying. Let's try it on a temporary basis. But if it doesn't work out, we will have to come up with some other arrangement.

WINOGRAD: Great!

□   □

STRATEGY

AFTER a decade of working to break through entry-level barriers to compete in full-fledged careers, women are now wondering how they can live dual lives—work and family. And, for the first time, we aren't alone in this situation. Men are also searching for balance. The B word is in now. Young husbands-turned-fathers don't want to duplicate their own fathers' obsessive work lives. But how can we avoid the trap?

If you think of the conflict between work and family as a time-management issue, there are always shortcuts to be found. Winograd could hire a nanny to care for her baby, manage her household, and do the cooking. She could buy a car phone to talk to her husband during her drive home. There are shortcuts available at the office, too. She could analyze her management process to ferret out places where she could reduce her workload, delegate more, and save time.

But while such tactics will help, they don't address the essence of the work-family dilemma, which confronts a large number of people in corporate America's huge and growing workforce. As a society, we haven't created any good models for combining family and work. The way most corporations are structured, it is essential that you give up your personal time to be successful. It's no accident that childless women fill most of the top corporate jobs held by women. One study found that only 35 percent of women executives under forty have children. That same study reported that 90 percent of male executives are fathers by the time they reach age forty. I'd be willing to bet that many of those executives have wives who don't work outside the home. The pattern has been set by the male CEO who is married to a devoted housewife and is essentially a bill-paying father.

The *Harvard Business Review* captured this tension in a recent study in which people were asked to state whether scenarios were good for the family or good for the organization. Seventy-five percent of the study's participants said a family member who stays home to take care of children is good for the family, but 65 percent thought it was good for the family that both spouses worked.

We are a society at odds with itself. And no matter how hard women work, the issue won't be resolved until we join forces to push hard for solutions to bridge the dichotomy of family *versus* work.

Until that happens, we have to work within the existing framework. That requires negotiating a situation that suits your specific needs. To do that, you first must answer the basic question Winograd is struggling with: Do you want a full or reduced work schedule?

There are plenty of reasons to choose a full load. If you stop or slow down your career to raise a family, you will have to deal with the inevitable problems associated with coming back: a loss of status and contacts and, frequently, fewer options. Like Winograd's friend Pat Fields, you will have to fight the perception that you are a mommy-tracker. Studies have shown that women who are able to manage the dual life raise independent children with a determined work ethic, although such women don't have as much free time as they would like. If Winograd chooses to continue her full-time schedule, she'll have to use more time-saving tactics, build a network of people to help care for her family (including a live-in housekeeper, perhaps with a college student to provide extra help), and accept the fact that she won't have the leisure time she'd like.

Of course, this situation doesn't suit everyone. If Winograd chooses a reduced schedule, she will need to work out a part-time schedule with her boss. Chances are he won't be thrilled, particularly if there is no precedent for such an arrangement at the organization. After all, even Winograd is disappointed by the decision made by Fields. Despite all of the evidence that working full-time doesn't make you more dedicated to your job, the perception is that part-time employees are less committed to their work. And in truth, some are. But that doesn't mean they will always be or that their part-time work isn't valuable. It just means that at this point in their career, work is taking a backseat to other concerns. Companies that recognize these employees' worth will look at a part-time position as an investment.

For Winograd the first issue is whether she herself can accept what working part-time will mean. The fact is, some people will see her as a mommy-tracker. And when she does come back to the organization full-time, she will have to work hard to win back the status and position she held previously. If she is willing to accept these consequences, then she needs to assess her standing in the organization before approaching her boss. Those who are new and relatively untried or who have fumbled their last few projects obviously will have less leverage. The best that they may be able to hope for is to reduce their workday to nine hours or to take a part-time position with a pro-rated pay cut minus benefits.

If Winograd has a good relationship with her boss, then she is in a much better negotiating position. But she still needs to recognize that part-time positions are new to most organizations. That means she has to anticipate every possible objection and be prepared to counter it. Before the meeting, she should rehearse with a friend. The more prepared she is, the better her chances. In fact, if her boss is partial to detailed plans, she might put her proposal in writing.

The ultimate challenge for Winograd will be in keeping her full-time status with a part-time job. I know a number of women who have managed to do this by holding on to the most prestigious projects and delegating the lesser ones. They also have taken care to keep up their contacts by continuing to lunch with colleagues and clients—and they have made sure that they didn't discuss their family. They've consciously presented themselves as the same ambitious and committed managers they always were.

If Winograd succeeds at this, she may also want to take on another challenge: restructuring her office to find a solution to the work-family conundrum. She could suggest starting a special task force to focus on this problem that affects so many men and women in her firm. The purpose of such a "brain trust" would be to research how progressive organizations are tackling the dilemma and to talk to experts in the area. In the short run, of course, championing this cause might cost her more time, the very thing she can least afford to give. But in taking on such a project she could solve a pressing problem which would undoubtedly bring her new career opportunities. It would also mean establishing a new bond between employer and employees, one that would allow her even more time with her husband, daughter, and second child.

SHOULD YOU
CHANGE YOUR JOB OR
YOUR CAREER?

If you're dissatisfied
and restless, you may need to do
something completely different.
Learn to read the signs.

Sarah Scott, a claims investigator for the state health department, has two opportunities before her. Her boss has offered her what is considered a plum assignment on a task force investigating blood-transfusion scams. In addition, a higher-paying supervisory position has opened up. Yet Scott feels unenthusiastic about both prospects and has taken action on neither.

Scott's attitude toward her work disturbs and mystifies her. In high school she was voted "Most Likely to Succeed" in honor of her academic achievements and her service as class treasurer, newspaper editor, debater, and hospital volunteer. In college she maintained her high level of extracurricular activity. And seven years ago, when she began working for the health department fresh out of graduate school, she was idealistic, eager, and driven.

But Scott, now thirty, finds herself struggling to make it through the workday. *Less* is the word that most accurately characterizes her work life: She talks about it less, thinks about it less, and reads about it less. She is beginning to suspect that her unrest may signify the need for a new job, or maybe even a new career.

No other jobs in the health department appeal to her. Her childhood dream of becoming a doctor has resurfaced recently, but she thinks it would be crazy to go back to school when she has a guaranteed career with fine benefits—four weeks' vacation, good medical coverage, and a livable pension. Not only is her job safe, but she can actually count on steady advancement, nothing to sneer at in these uncertain times. Yet she cringes at the realization of what her ambition has been reduced to—a passion for a pension.

☐   # SWITCHING GEARS   ☐

Finding a challenging job or career requires drive, time, soul searching, and hard work. The following are some avenues to explore (simultaneously).

- Investigate higher-ranking, higher-paying jobs within your company. Using whatever contacts you have, meet with the people who hold these jobs. Find out what they do and what you need to do to land a similar job.
- Search for more interesting jobs in other companies. Again, talk to those who hold such jobs. For sources, read directories and journals and attend lectures and seminars.
- Consider jumping over the fence and working for the other side. Scott, for example, might want to consider a job with a pharmaceutical company or a hospital. You may find that this is the best option, because it enables you to use skills you've already acquired, but in a challenging new environment.
- Examine unrealized dreams—careers you've secretly wished you could have and professionals you've admired

or even envied. Find out what's involved in realizing those dreams; for instance, in which areas do you need more experience?

• Send for diverse graduate school catalogs. Apply to every program that appeals to you. To give yourself as many options as possible, apply to the best programs, regardless of the cost (loans, scholarships, and fellowships are often available), and also apply to those that offer night classes or give credit for past courses or life experience.

• Keep a notebook to record each meeting; note who, when, what was promised, your reaction. Review it weekly to keep up with what you've initiated. And stay positive. Remind yourself that you are working to catapult yourself into a new area where you will best be able to use your talents.

☐   ☐

STRATEGY

I empathize completely with Scott. When I was twenty-eight I had a similar conflict. I was a teacher and desperately wanted to leave my profession, but I was afraid of giving up my secure position. I have let myself risk changing my career not once but three times since then, and I've never felt as old as I did when I was twenty-eight.

My experience isn't unusual, according to *Workplace 2000: The Revolution Reshaping American Business.* The authors, Joseph Bayett and Henry Conn, suggest that the average American beginning his or her career in the 1990s will probably work in ten or more jobs for five or more employers before retiring. In fact, I've noticed that most of my clients hit turning points every decade of their lives. Scott is right on schedule: The end of the twenties often marks the first significant career reevaluation. That is when people's true selves—their preferences, talents, interests, flaws, and dreams—begin to emerge.

Up to that point most people follow the dictates of parents, friends, mentors, and spouses. It's a formula that works for some: Slipping into others' programs as if into a ready-made dress, they said the fit was perfect. Others are even luckier: They recognize their talents right off the bat and base careers on them. But most people find their true calling only after spending a few years in the workforce. Bringing her true self into focus, then, should be Scott's goal.

She already knows she has to change her job or her career—she just doesn't know which. Since both the possibility of a special project and the opportunity to advance depress her, it's obvious that the problem is complex. She needs something different, not just more of the same.

Scott should look not only to change her work but also to reclaim herself. She started out as a leader, building on her talents, interests, and intelligence. Yet at the end of her twenties none of that leadership and passion is apparent in her work life. She has lost sight of what she can do and what she wants to do. She has repressed her dreams and her ambitions.

Only Scott knows for sure why she has denied her ambitions, but it is a common phenomenon among women. I see it in my clients. And Harvard professor Carol Gilligan has described a similar pattern: In her research she found that strong, bright, and confident girls live out full lives in their early years but start reining themselves in as adolescents, when they are faced with enormous pressure to conform to stereotypical notions of femininity.

On some level Scott may have chosen to work for the government partly out of a desire for job security; only she can sort out her motivations. Her task now is to explore other options, regardless of the risks. She should start by assessing herself. What does she like and dislike about her current job? Is there anyone, inside or outside her company, whose job she would like to have in five or ten years? Which tasks does she perform most and least successfully? She should rank each item on a scale of one to ten, then compile a list of other duties she would like to undertake. Through this exercise she will see patterns emerge, and she should be able to identify jobs or careers centered on them.

Scott needs to be realistic and consider the sacrifices required in changing careers. Many career switches involve accepting a position of lesser rank or pay. But I wouldn't advise her—or anyone else—to dismiss a career for that reason. After all, we pay universities tuition for the chance to learn. Why not accept a lower-paying job for the same purpose? If Scott discovers that she wants to realize her old dream and enroll in medical school, she should consider that option as well. While it's true that she's already thirty now, she's going to be thirty-six someday anyway; why not be thirty-six with a medical degree and an internship under her belt, and a residency just ahead?

One definition of courage is a willingness to try new ventures despite their costs. Any career change Scott contemplates will probably involve sacrifice, some of it onerous. Which one she chooses is up to her. But if she can allow herself to become an enthusiastic explorer of her career path, she will be rewarded with more than just a better job. She'll have a fulfilling career.

How Ambitious
Are You?

<blockquote>
If moving up
makes you nervous, you
need to tackle your fear
and aim higher.
</blockquote>

Donna Stockman has been fascinated by what she calls high-tech food ever since she watched NASA astronauts land on the moon and dine on freeze-dried turkey and dressing. Now a biochemist with a leading manufacturer of food and chemical products, Stockman is living her dream. She has assisted in the development of several profitable high-tech products. Her team's latest research hit the jackpot, coming up with a low-calorie substitute for fat. Making people thin will make the company even richer. But guiding the product's development isn't the only opportunity before her.

Two weeks ago her boss resigned, leaving open the position of senior biochemist. Rumor has it that a search committee is looking for a replacement within the company, and half a dozen people have already thrown their hats in the ring.

Stockman knows she is well qualified for the job. She is probably the most skilled biochemist in the department. Yet she is hesitant to act. She had secretly hoped that management would just offer her the job—then she wouldn't have to make the decision to apply for it and face the uncertain consequences.

Moving up makes her nervous. She envisions a host of problems. What if she were to apply and be rejected? Would management (and her new boss) write her off as being a little too eager for her own good? What if she gets the job and finds that she can't handle it? Would she be able to live with the failure? And suppose she does succeed? Then she would have to deal with the anger and jealousy of her co-workers, who would almost certainly resent her becoming their boss.

If she were promoted, she would have to work longer hours and travel more. The salary increase would be nice, but she is at a safe plateau; why go for the steeper learning curve? Is it worth jeopardizing her happiness for a few hundred dollars more a month?

When Stockman talked to her husband about the job, he encouraged her to go for it. "It's what you want," he said. "That's always been your ambition." He's right—she's always had her eye on the job of senior biochemist. She knows she should aim for the top. But she is afraid of the costs.

☐ ELEVEN SIGNS THAT YOU'RE VEERING OFF-TRACK ☐

Ambition inspires people to want more than they have and to dare to strive for it. But some people, fearful of failure, repress their aspirations. Here are eleven indications that you may have a problem.

- You find yourself envious of others' accomplishments and fantasize about being in their shoes.
- You read about your industry in trade periodicals but don't take action on the ideas your reading generates.

- You know who the key players in your organization are, as well as in the competition, but you don't make the time or the effort to get to know them.
- You feel like you're selling out if you assume a high profile but are disappointed in yourself when you find you are adopting a passive role.
- You frequently second-guess your boss's decisions and feel resentful about following his or her direction.
- You feel energized listening to those who are senior to you but feel depressed that you aren't one of them.
- You have given up taking big risks.
- You don't entertain your co-workers and superiors at home because you feel inadequate at social gatherings.
- You blame the recession, office politics, or fate for your status.
- You scorn those who are successfully living out their ambitions.
- You socialize primarily with those who lack ambition.

STRATEGY

WHAT prevents people from using their skills, realizing their potential, and taking their place among those who are equally talented? The answer may lie in the word Stockman chokes on: ambition.

In the aftermath of the eighties, many people, like Stockman, are under the impression that "ambition" is a negative trait. Of course, some ambitious people have a dark side and can be so driven by a desire for money, power, or fame that they are willing to back-stab, lie, and even steal to get what they want. But I would argue that this is due not so much to their aspirations as their character flaws. Ambition does not require insider trading; corruption does.

For most people ambition is a positive force, fanning the fires of their passions and inspiring them to create and achieve. An enormous commitment of time and energy is required to satisfy ambition. But the payoff is responsibility, challenge, and advancement.

Women, unfortunately, have been conditioned to repress their dreams. Taught to be "nice," they put other people's needs and feelings before their own. As a result, they shun confrontation and avoid putting themselves in situations where they will dominate and be highly visible. They do not boast or show off. They keep a low profile, faithfully serving as the handmaid, never the star.

To fulfill your ambition, you must be willing to start to assert your desires over others' and take the risk of placing yourself in tense, contentious situations. Stockman instinctively senses and fears this possibility, so she tries to deny her own drive, which makes her feel frustrated and depressed.

She needs to wage and win her internal war against ambition. If a job is a box, then Stockman has spilled over the sides. She's ready for more. She must recognize her dreams, present from the time she was a child, and strive to realize them, or later she may regret having limited herself.

Stockman is correct in one crucial respect: Launching her campaign for the newly vacated senior biochemist position will be risky. No one knows what the outcome will be. The only way to tackle her fear, though, is to acknowledge it and plunge ahead anyway. While lobbying for this position requires steeling herself, possibly for a bruising battle, the process of doing so will build courage.

Stockman's primary anxiety is that she will fail. Obviously, the fear of failing is a complex syndrome, relating to many factors, including a lack of self-confidence. Both men and women suffer from it, but I have noticed that for some women the syndrome is related to their fear of letting someone down. As part of their good-girl training, they prefer to gracefully decline a new assignment rather than risk not being able to deliver; men are generally more likely to feel they have earned the new assignment.

To overcome this fear, Stockman should approach trusted colleagues and mentors, especially those who are women, and discuss the pros and cons of competing for the job. She needs to hear their experiences so that she will be realistic about the process. There's no denying that she will feel rejected and deflated if she doesn't get the job, but like others who don't get what they want, she will have to learn to smile publicly, show complete support for the new manager, and serve as a loyal assistant—until there is another opening in the company's upper ranks.

And if she gets the position? Stockman will have to face the challenge of mastering new tasks and expanding her network to include other senior managers. That will be hard work, but most of my clients—women like Stockman—thrive on the challenge of using their creativity and accumulated knowledge, and are rewarded for their efforts with success and increased confidence.

But Stockman should not delude herself. Ambitious women face obstacles that men do not. Some people undoubtedly will be threatened by her success. They may not like her as much as they did before. They may even seek revenge by sabotaging her efforts to perform well in her new job. When women step out of the traditional role of serving others and into the role of leader, they are sometimes punished. They are labeled bitches or, worse, rumored to be sleeping their way to the top.

If that happens to Stockman and she knows who the culprits are, she should confront them and try to elicit their support, or at least a truce, by pointing out that they need to work together to be successful. If she doesn't know who is behind the rumors, she will have to do what women before her have done: recognize the gossip as a product of jealousy and move on. As for the "friends" she loses, that, unfortunately, is a cost of rising to the top. Once you stop being one of the gang and become the leader, relationships will change.

Recently there have been many articles about high-powered professionals who drop off the fast track by choice, often to raise children. Can unambitious people be happy? Absolutely. Most likely they are channeling their creativity into other areas—family, hobbies, community activities. Once their children become more independent, however, many women return to pursue their careers actively again.

Everyone has a need to learn, grow, and have his or her talents recognized and rewarded. And, increasingly, women are learning the lessons that men have always been taught—the bigger the risk the greater the reward.

INTERVIEWING
FOR THE TOP

> The higher you go,
> the tougher the questions
> get. How to handle them
> like a pro.

Terry Young's spirits sank as she read the rejection letter from the president of a small boutique bank. Not ony is the job—chief financial officer—a fine position, but Young, a director of systems development at a larger bank, has been counting on it to extricate her from an unpleasant situation.

One long year ago Young was brought in as the heir apparent to the information-systems vice president. The senior officers who hired her told her that she would take over the vice president's post as soon as she proved she was familiar with the bank's systems and a suitable new job was found for her boss. They said the VP wasn't working out and assured her that the move would take place within four months.

Everyone knew the plan, even the vice president himself, who claimed to welcome a transfer. As the year passed, however, and as Young's strengths became obvious, her boss dug in his heels and clung to his position. And top management buckled under. Recently they informed her that they could not find an appropriate spot for him and that she would have to stay put for a while.

Fortuitously, she got a call from a headhunter about the CFO position just when she had decided to start looking for a new job. Having long ago read the books on how to ace an interview, Young did everything she was supposed to do. She researched the job and the bank's position in the industry. During the interview she spoke positively about her boss, her job, and the organization. She rattled off the polished, pat responses to the inevitable questions. When the president and senior vice president asked why she wanted to leave her job, she gave the ready-made answer—more challenges and greater rewards. Then they asked her what it was she wanted to do and why she couldn't accomplish it where she was. They kept probing. Flustered, Young lost her nerve and began stammering. When they got around to talking about a financial package, they suggested she start at the low end of the range, saying she had never held the title of CFO before. Her confidence shaken, Young didn't counter.

Now Young has received written confirmation that she failed, flubbed the interview—a first for her. Not only is it humiliating, but it means she is stuck in a job she hates.

□ TRICK QUESTIONS, □
TRICKIER ANSWERS

Here are three popular interview questions, along with the right and wrong responses, and explanations of why they do and don't work. While you will need to tailor your answers to match your situation, these can serve as a guide.

Why do you want to leave your current job?

WRONG RESPONSE: I want more challenges and greater rewards. I have highly developed skills that aren't being fully used.

RIGHT RESPONSE: I was hired last year with the understanding that I would be promoted within a year. But because of a reorganization and subsequent turf battles, the bank has decided not to expand the department. They told me that I will have to stay put for a while. Based on what I see, it could be a year before they resume their expansion plans. After much thought, I've come to the conclusion that it would be best for me to leave. I don't know if you've ever been in this kind of situation, but it's tough.

EXPLANATION: The question is open-ended and invites discussion. The first answer is glib. The second one, however, is candid without being backbiting, and may prompt further conversation.

What kind of compensation are you looking for?

WRONG RESPONSE: I need a salary of about $95,000, but it's negotiable.

RIGHT RESPONSE: I'd prefer that you make an offer, but I do need three provisions: a bonus; a change-in-control contract since you alluded to a possible takeover; and finally, the usual one-year severance agreement with an up-front guarantee.

EXPLANATION: You should never show your hand before they do, but if pushed to say something, make sure you request what other senior officers have. That will demonstrate that you are their peer.

I see you've also worked with John Rogers. How was that?

WRONG RESPONSE: Not very pleasant, I'm afraid. He was extremely difficult to work with, but perhaps he's changed.

RIGHT RESPONSE: John? Of course. I worked with him in my early days at the bank. So you know him? Small world, isn't it? Did you work with him, too?

EXPLANATION: Since you don't know their relationship, why risk responding negatively? If pressed, you can smile and say he was quite the perfectionist.

☐   ☐

STRATEGY

CAREER books always tell you that interviews help you determine whether you're compatible with your prospective employer and set the tone for that relationship. But what many books don't tell you is exactly the lesson that Young learned: When you enter the executive ranks, the rules become considerably more complex.

Look at what happened to Young. She applied the conventional wisdom—be positive about the past and chant "challenge" for the future—and found that this advice, which had worked so well for junior positions, failed miserably. Why? Because the interviewers wanted to see whether she could fill a CFO's shoes, not a middle manager's. They wanted to know if she was perceptive and analytical enough to handle a top job, so they asked tough, probing questions. Young's simplistic answers did not satisfy them, but the truth—or at least some portion of it—would have.

What do you reveal and how do you protect yourself? How do you deal with the politically sensitive questions you will undoubtedly be asked, starting with "Why do you want to leave your job?" First, you must never badmouth your boss or top management, or show anger—that reflects poorly on your professionalism. Second, you should dictate the agenda, not the interviewer. Think about a politician being interviewed by a TV host. No matter what question is asked, the pol will convey the message he wants to get across. Many times he won't even answer the question. If he is intelligent and personable enough, no one notices.

In job interviews, of course, employers won't be satisfied unless their bottom-line question is answered: "Are you enough like us to join our club?" For senior-level positions, they also want to know whether the applicant is sophisticated and smart enough to handle the job. But as long as these underlying concerns are addressed, interviewers, like the TV host, can easily be diverted.

When Young was asked why she wanted to leave her job, she should have responded by initiating a dialogue on management issues. She could have started by explaining the circumstances under which she was hired and then analyzed how her boss's style impedes not only her work but also the department's. (By speaking dispassionately and being politic in her description of her boss's shortcomings, she would not have sounded critical, but perceptive and honest.) She might then have asked her interviewers whether they had encountered a similar problem and what actions they had taken to resolve it. Young then could have led the discussion toward how bankers in senior management should deal with ineffectual managers. Through her response, she would have demonstrated her intellectual and analytical skills and forged a connection.

Of course, if her interviewers had seemed conservative and reserved, then she would not have wanted to stray far from the keep-it-positive approach. Every job applicant, particularly one seeking a top post, needs to read the verbal and nonverbal messages interviewers send out. Young's error lay in failing to see that her interviewers' provocative questions called for provocative answers.

What about interviewers who don't give you a chance to sell yourself? Should you interrupt and make them listen? Absolutely not. You must interpret the behavior and recognize it as a need to play leader. Perhaps no one listens to them in their offices, so they are seizing a captive audience. Or maybe they just always need to be in control. Whatever the reason, they want to be the talkers. Don't interrupt or show any irritation. Instead, at the end of the interview, praise their ingenuity and knowledge, thank them for sharing their experience with you, and relate an instance of your own that complements theirs. They may not be able to remember your job history, but most likely they will recall how much they liked you. As for your questions, get them answered elsewhere—through the grapevine, printed company material, or a second or third interview.

There is one caveat. Do not try to read your interviewer when it comes to broaching politically sensitive subjects; it's too dangerous. If you absolutely must know about the company's fiscal status or failing product, the safest approach is to lead into it by asking for a reaction to a currently circulated news story or rumor rather than being offensively direct.

If you should discover that the company is facing financial troubles, you could negotiate for a one-year severance agreement, guaranteed up front. And if they offer you a salary at the low end of the scale, as happened to Young, you could counter with a fair compromise: If you meet their expectations, you will be given, say, a 25 percent bonus. Far from being offended that you are asking for too much, prospective employers will be convinced that you are only seeking what they would require for themselves—and that you're right for the job.

MOVING OVER
INSTEAD OF UP

A *horizontal move
can boost your career or
stall it. Here's how to
tell the difference.*

Joan Ross isn't sure whether she should be excited or depressed. Nearly a year ago, Ross, a manager in the audit department of a midsize accounting firm, began aggressively job hunting, bored with her job. No positions materialized, but yesterday she did receive an offer to work in her own firm's most important department—tax. Not only would the position give her experience in a critical area, but she would be reporting directly to a highly respected partner who, by all accounts, makes an effort to mentor his managers. However, the job has a few negatives. She would keep her current title and receive slightly lower pay than she gets now. "Keep looking," a friend counseled her. "You can find a real promotion. You're good."

The fact is, though, this is the first appealing offer she's received. And the personnel officer who referred her assured her that the move would not be looked upon as a demotion. "This is a partner-track job," she said.

Since few firms are hiring now, Ross could easily wait another two years before a senior-management position opens up else-where—during which time she would die of boredom. Having been in her job for five years, she has learned all she can. And although she is well regarded by the senior managers in her own department, she won't be promoted until one of them is made partner, which isn't going to happen anytime soon. These days, the firm wants to cut back on the audit department, not add to it.

The tax manager's position could be a great opportunity for Ross to be exposed to a hot, growing field. She wants to grab it, but she worries: Would making a lateral move mark her as me-diocre, someone who couldn't find a "real" promotion? Would she be taking a step down?

STRATEGY

UNTIL recently, most advice on career development focused on how to move up the corporate ladder. The thinking was that only the inferior moved sideways; horizontal moves connoted stagnation or failure. All that changed in the late 1980s, as corporate America began a series of cutbacks and layoffs that resulted in a broader, flatter hierarchy. Lateral moves were no longer taboo, and were even encouraged; some Fortune 500 companies began using them as a way to keep valued employees chal-lenged and motivated.

In fact, one of the trends in the personnel business is a new horizontal structure called "broad banding," in which employees are loosely organized into a few broad job categories, rather than dozens of titles in traditional systems. Such a system encourages employees to focus on developing skills instead of following the old-fashioned linear path of advancement.

In a recent survey of 2,006 large companies by the benefits-consulting firm Hewitt Associates, just 6 percent reported broad banding, but a whopping 35 percent said they are considering implementing such a structure. Clearly, the stigma associated with horizontal moves is waning.

But Ross is right to be leery of accepting a job that offers her no improvement in salary or rank. Some employers do use horizontal moves as a way to shove employees out the door. And some managers view employees who take such transfers as deadwood. Ross has been assured by the personnel department that this isn't the case, but she needs to go a step further in investigating. She should have frank discussions with the tax partner, other senior executives in the firm, and possibly even her current boss (if she has a good relationship with him or her) to find out whether the job would really enhance her standing. If they were in her place, would they wait for something better?

A lateral move often involves compromise in salary or title. To compensate, the job has to offer great training, experience, or exposure. You must be convinced that the position will help you develop valuable skills that will make you more marketable for your next big move. In Ross's case, the tax manager's position would do all that and more—providing her with the opportunity to make a powerful ally.

I usually advise my clients to conduct a thorough job search for a few months before making a lateral move so that they can better assess the offer. Ross has done this, and has come to the conclusion that the new job is truly a step up from what she has now.

Does she need to convince others of that fact? In business, perception can be reality. She can't let the impression be created that she settled for a lesser position. She has to respond, briefly but confidently, to remarks like the one her friend made. She could say, for instance, "I've been eager to move to tax for a long time, and working directly for the partner was an opportunity I couldn't pass up." She might add that many companies today invest in their best employees by rotating their assignments.

Those who accept a horizontal move to a competitor may

have to fight the perception that they left their company because they were forced out. Rather than badmouthing your former boss in such a situation, talk up the virtues of your new employer ("I was really impressed with the company's consistent growth and the way it develops its employees"). Few would dispute the importance of working at a prosperous company.

Today, career paths often follow a zigzag pattern. Sometimes you will follow a straight, vertical line, sometimes you'll move sideways. What's important is to make sure that each move adds to your knowledge, preparing you for your next job. If you do, you will discover that a lateral move can help you make a bigger leap than you expected.

MAKING THE MOST
OF YOUR REVIEW

It's time to sell yourself. Making a good case at a performance evaluation can improve working relationships and set the stage for advancement.

Although her performance review is weeks away, Michelle Gold, a manager for a major public-relations firm, is worried. A recent round of budget cuts forced her to lay off one of her two assistants this year. She and her remaining staffer have worked hard to maintain their clients, and—quite remarkably, Gold thinks—they have succeeded. But their work has suffered in other areas.

Two of Gold's most recent projects were flops. A publicity campaign for a cosmetics account she manages failed to attract any national press attention. Then she bungled a follow-up presentation. Fortunately her performance didn't seem to cause any long-term damage; the company is still willing to work with her.

But Gold fears that her boss, Dennis Leeds, a perfectionist, will not be so understanding during the review process. Already he has made a few cutting remarks to her. "We can't afford mistakes," he said last week when she tried to explain why she had forgotten to send him a copy of a fax from a prospective client.

After logging sixty-hour weeks for a year and running her department on a shoestring, Gold hopes—and expects—that she will receive a significant raise this year. What if Leeds says she doesn't deserve one? One of her co-workers tried to comfort her by telling her that she was placing too much emphasis on the appraisal process. "Leeds hates that kind of thing. He sees them as busywork for the paper pushers," the colleague said, adding, "Besides, he's probably decided how much of a raise you're going to get anyway."

But Gold doesn't want to leave anything to chance. To alleviate her anxieties, she has decided to prepare herself for the review, mapping out possible responses to Leeds's criticisms of her. Still, she wonders if her colleague isn't right. Hasn't Leeds already made up his mind? Could she really do or say anything at this point to change his opinion of her?

□ ## WHAT THEY SAY, □
WHAT THEY MEAN

Reviewers rarely come right out and say what they want to know. Instead, they try to mask questions in benign phrases. Here we decode some standard performance-review questions and offer tips for responding to them.

How would you assess your performance at work this year?
TRANSLATION: *Do you see yourself clearly—i.e., exactly the way I see you?*

Acknowledge whatever shortcomings your boss may have pointed out to you in the past; that will impress him or her and allow for more openness between you. Then make sure to turn the conversation to your talents so that your positive assessment is highlighted.

What are your strengths and skills?
TRANSLATION: *What do you really bring to this company?*
Here's your chance to sell yourself. If you have trouble singing
  your own praises, imagine what you wish your boss would
  say about you; then repeat it.

In which areas do you most want to improve?
TRANSLATION: *Can we really count on you to become
  the kind of executive we want?*
Begin by admitting to some of your recent failings. Indicate
  concern—not remorse or shame; that will only detract
  from your professionalism. Emphasize how you rectified
  the situation and what steps you have taken to ensure
  that the same mistakes will not happen again.

*What jobs or tasks would you like to see yourself take on
next?*
TRANSLATION: *How ambitious are you?*
This is your opportunity to let your manager know what your
  goals are. Detail the specific contributions you've made,
  and be specific about how you want to advance, in terms
  of both job title and areas of responsibility. Then explain
  how this would contribute to the company's future, as
  well as to your boss's plans.

STRATEGY

PERFORMANCE reviews are a relatively new phenomenon,
a direct response to the exponential growth in lawsuits filed—or
threatened—by employees. In an effort to protect themselves
against claims of wrongful termination and age, sex, and racial
discrimination, organizations are trying to shore up their docu-

mentation. As a result, written evaluations have become de rigueur.

Nearly every major corporation now uses some kind of ratings form, ranging from perfunctory checklists to detailed, handwritten assessments that run on for pages. There are even consultants who specialize in performance reviews and professional associations, like the Human Resource Planning Society in New York, that often hold planning sessions on them.

Most employees approach the performance-review process like Gold, with dread and the sinking feeling that it is all for naught. They don't realize that reviews can provide them with more than just an opportunity for self-defense; if handled properly, they can dramatically enhance work relationships and set the stage for advancement. While it's true that Gold's boss has already formed an opinion of her, it is also true that his opinion can be changed. Gold needs to use the same techniques that she would use to land a new account: persuasion, careful listening, and flattery. The review is the time to sell yourself—make a good case and you will be amply rewarded.

To her credit, Gold already recognizes the need to prepare for the meeting. But before actually working out her responses, she should consider the circumstances of the appraisal. In a group review, for instance, where an employee meets with and is assessed by a group of supervisors, it's wise to keep answers as upbeat as possible. A complaint from a staffer, no matter how well couched, is likely to be seen as a challenge by the managers, who will be quick to join forces and defend themselves.

The majority of companies, however, use one-on-one reviews. Here the most pressing question becomes, what is the *real* agenda of the meeting? You need to find out from your co-workers how their appraisals were conducted. In the worst-case scenario, the evaluation is wrapped around an ax and is part of a hidden plan to reduce the staff. In that event, you need to brace yourself for an attack and try to respond calmly. Request written documentation and a chance to defend yourself. But don't expect to change your boss's mind; the decision probably came from the very top. Your aim should be to buy as much time as possible in which to find another job.

Most of the time, managers don't have ulterior motives. Usually they dislike the review process as much as their staff does. Having little experience in, or stomach for, dealing with face-to-face confrontations, some may even view them as a burden. Gold's friend has indicated that Leeds doesn't put much credence in the process. That doesn't mean, however, that Gold shouldn't. She can still get what she wants out of the experience—a raise—if she presents her skills and achievements persuasively enough.

Gold should rehearse by writing down her accomplishments. That will force her to examine herself closely and will enable her to speak calmly and with authority during the review. I would wait until the actual meeting, however, to decide whether to give a copy of the self-evaluation memo to Leeds. During the meeting, she should sniff out Leeds's attitude and act accordingly. If he seems to take the evaluation lightly, then she should either forget about giving him the memo or offer to give him a copy at a later point and see if he responds well. If Leeds doesn't seem eager for her memo, she should simply not give it to him.

Since Gold wants a substantial raise, she has to prove that she has gone way beyond the call of duty. If Leeds doesn't initiate a discussion of her accomplishments, she should lead the conversation to that subject. She must inform him not only of the goals she met but also of how she reached them, what else she hopes for, and how ready and eager she is for even bigger challenges. She also might ask Leeds what he thinks should be the next step in her career. If he doesn't respond directly, she can state what she would like to see herself doing during the next few years; in this way, she will lay the ground work for it.

Under no circumstances should Gold invite an extensive discussion of her shortcomings, but if her worst fear is realized and Leeds attacks her for botching the cosmetics campaign, she should acknowledge her mistakes, apologize for them, and explain the steps she has taken to ensure they won't ever happen again. She must not be defensive or belabor the topic—that would only signal immaturity and lack of professionalism. More than likely, a swift apology will disarm her boss and close the subject forever. If not, she could try another approach and solicit his advice: Was he ever in a similar situation? If so, how did he handle it? What does he think she needs to do to remedy her problem?

Whether Leeds criticizes her or not, Gold should end the meeting by thanking him for his effort. Don't forget that conducting an evaluation, especially a thorough one, can be taxing, too. Gold needs to let Leeds know how much she appreciates and values his input. That will end the review on a positive note and reinforce the message that the appraisal was not simply a grading session but a time to work together and plan for her future.

SECOND-STAGE
MENTORING

> At *mid-career you*
> *still need an adviser*
> *and ally—but of a*
> *different sort.*

Ruth Johnston, a thirty-seven-year-old publicity director at a public utility, feels stranded. For the past dozen years, whenever she had a problem she had only to walk down the hall and talk it over with Bruce Brill, the senior vice president in charge of corporate communications. Brill, who had hired Johnston as his assistant, would always take the time to support, direct, and encourage his protégé.

But recently Johnston began to feel increasingly uncomfortable going to Brill for guidance. Either he would suggest solutions she had already thought of and knew wouldn't work, or the tables would turn and she would end up advising *him* on sticky political situations. Johnston had, in fact, not only caught up with Brill but surpassed him, thanks in part to his diligent tutelage. A few months ago, when the higher-ups began edging Brill out of his job, Johnston gave him some leads for a position with another firm. Last month, when the job finally materialized, Brill took it and left.

Johnston is now without a mentor—at the time she needs one most. She has reached a career crossroads: Having been a publicity director for three years, she is restless and anxious to move up. Brill tried to help her, but his own position was too precarious. Johnston knew she wouldn't be promoted into Brill's spot without a strong advocate at the top, so she tried to befriend Sally Keller, the only female senior vice president, but Keller rebuffed her overtures. Johnston needs another, more experienced version of Brill to help her make her next move, but she doesn't see any prospects. She wonders: At her age, can she hope to find another mentor?

☐ # A GUIDE TO ☐
FINDING GUIDANCE

By the time you reach mid-level management, you no longer need a mentor so much as a group of savvy professionals with whom you can exchange ideas and contacts. What follows are seven tips for developing this network.

- Start a file on women and men whose work you admire. Set a goal of becoming friendly with at least one or two of them.
- Become active in one or more professional, civic, or advocacy groups that deal with issues in which you are interested. Assume a leadership role on a committee or task force.
- Make a special effort to build relationships with successful women in your field. Their war stories will help you cope with the sexism that, unfortunately, is still rampant in the corporate world.

- Arrange a lunch with a few colleagues, then try to turn it into a monthly event during which you can discuss career issues.
- Solidify relationships by entertaining regularly. Celebrate holidays, birthdays, and promotions with co-workers, peers, and superiors in and out of your field.
- Demonstrate your appreciation for the talents of business friends and acquaintances. Through calls or notes, congratulate those who have been promoted, started new businesses, or won awards.
- Be generous with your time and knowledge. Share information. Help lift up those below you, particularly women. One day they may repay the favor.

☐ ☐

STRATEGY

JOHNSTON should applaud herself. She did exactly what she should have done in the early stages of her career. She found a manager to coach and champion her. With his help, she made her way into the ranks of middle management and, quite naturally, became his equal. Her problem is common to mid-career professionals. The protégé often outgrows the mentor and faces two uncomfortable feelings: guilt and fear. Having lost the person who was her cheerleader and guide, she suddenly finds herself alone—and in the position of unwittingly showing up the person who has supported and helped her.

In some ways, Johnston is lucky. Brill left before they wound up pitted against each other. But she is also right in seeing that she needs to find a replacement for him in order to advance further inside or outside the company.

At this stage of her career, though, she needs an entirely

different kind of adviser. In the beginning, you need someone older and wiser to help you figure out the basics: what to do, how to do it, what to say, and when. But as you move up, the decisions you need to make are not only more complex but more varied. With your expertise and responsibilities increasing, you need fewer explanations and lessons and more strategy suggestions and introductions.

In fact, middle managers usually don't rely on one person for this kind of feedback. Instead they develop a network of people who have gone through similar experiences and can act as sounding boards for them. Unlike the early career mentor, who is typically a superior found within your own company, mid-career mentors are often peers, and some are even in other fields. In fact, the more ambitious you are, the greater the range of your contacts needs to be. Think of mid-career mentors as your own brain trust—your personal board of directors.

Of course, since Johnston wants a promotion, she should first try again to develop allies within her company. Other senior officers in her firm may have kept their distance because she was identified as Brill's protégé when he was out of favor. If she makes an effort to cultivate them now, she may find them more receptive.

How to do that? Johnston should start by identifying one or two executives she would like to befriend and then letting them know that she appreciates what they do well. Other senior-level women, especially if upper-level management is largely male, aren't necessarily the best choices; sometimes they perceive only a certain number of slots for women in the company and feel threatened. Once Johnston chooses the people she wants to pursue, a good opener would be to compliment them on a program, project, or speech they gave, then initiate a conversation about how they managed to put it together so successfully. If she applies any of their strategies, she should report back her results and ask them for further input.

Even if she succeeds at building some relationships, she needs to widen her network outside the company. No one should be dependent on the goodwill of a few office mates. She might consider becoming active in professional, political, or civic associations, and women's groups are among the best places to make lasting connections. Not only will they expand the contacts you've made in your field, but they will also widen your network.

Johnston might also form her own informal women's group. Many women I know have standing breakfast or lunch dates once a month or so, without any agenda other than talking about what is happening in their careers. The higher you go in the corporate hierarchy, the more you will treasure these kinds of relationships. As you begin to find yourself among the few women at the top, you will draw comfort from hearing how other women deal with the sexism and the isolation. Even Lucie Salhany, who as chair of Twentieth Century Television is one of the few Hollywood women with the power to "green-light" projects, makes a point of having dinner with a handful of other women VIPs, including Dawn Steel, former head of Columbia Pictures, and Kay Koplovitz, President and CEO of USA Networks. "It makes me sad that there are so few of us," says Salhany, obviously savoring her relationships with other high-level women.

To form such alliances, Johnston will have to be willing to give, not just take. Now that she is in a position of influence, a number of people—not only Brill—will expect her to reciprocate favors. She will have to share ideas and contacts; no one's interested in a one-way relationship.

She should also start looking *down* the ladder in her organization for bright up-and-comers to coach. It's unfortunate that the senior woman, Sally Keller, hasn't set the tone by mentoring her and others, but Johnston must not join that small but hurtful minority of women who, despite having made it, are too insecure or self-involved to extend their hands to others on the way up. Such women often mistakenly think that aligning themselves with other women will make them look weak or diminish their stature, when in fact the opposite is true. As Muriel Siebert, the first woman to buy a seat on the New York Stock Exchange, recently said in an interview with the *New York Times*, women will never gain parity in the business world until they begin to help each other. "Lawsuits won't do it," said Siebert. "It will take the decided effort on the part of major firms to make sure that women are advanced according to their abilities. And it will be up to the women who rise to the top to see that they make that effort."

Not only does Johnston owe it to her younger "sisters," but it makes good business sense. For as Brill could tell her, mentors need their protégés for many reasons—not least because one day they may become their best allies.

About the Author

Adele Scheele is an internationally recognized career strategist for organizations and individuals wanting to succeed. She presents keynote addresses, seminars, and retreats for corporations, professional associations, and educational institutions. Dr. Scheele also coaches individuals to discover their callings, resolve their career dilemmas, and realize their goals.

Adele Scheele writes the career strategies column for *Working Woman* magazine. She has also written *Skills for Success* and *Making College Pay Off* (Ballantine). She has appeared on the "Today" show and "Good Morning America" as a career expert and on KABC talk radio as host. She earned a Ph.D. from UCLA as a Change Management Fellow, her master's degree in English from the California State University at Northridge, and her bachelor's degree from the University of Pennsylvania.

For information about career and change management,
contact Adele Scheele at:
225 West 83rd Street
New York, NY 10024
(212) 769-0654
Fax: (212) 769-0343